HAWAII'S HUMPBACK WHALES

HAWAII'S HUMPBACK WHALES

A COMPLETE WHALEWATCHERS GUIDE

by
Gregory Dean Kaufman
and
Paul Henry Forestell

PACIFIC WHALE FOUNDATION PRESS

The PACIFIC WHALE FOUNDATION, founded in 1980, is an international non-profit, tax-exempt organization dedicated to the study and preservation of marine mammals and their habitat. The Pacific Whale Foundation and its members have worked internationally to research and implement conservation programs on behalf of marine mammals. Through its publishing program, PACIFIC WHALE FOUNDATION PRESS, the Foundation offers books, technical reports, and a quarterly journal in the hope of expanding the public's understanding of the Pacific Whale Foundation—its concerns, goals, and objectives. The point of view expressed in each publication, however, does not necessarily represent the views of the Pacific Whale Foundation. For information on how you can help the whales, dolphins and other marine mammals or become involved in the research programs of the Foundation, please write to PACIFIC WHALE FOUNDATION, Post Office Box 1038, Kihei, Maui, Hawaii 96753.

Library of Congress Catalog Card Number:
86-61055
ISBN: 0-938725-00-9

Gregory D. Kaufman, executive editor.
Design, photoset and preparation by Studio Maui,
Richard P. Wirtz, art director.
Printed and bound in New Zealand.

Never, never doubt what
no one's sure about.

Gene Wilder in Willie Wonka and the Chocolate Factory

For
Kristi, Cathy, Jordan and Makena

Table of Contents

List of Tables

CHARTS, MAPS AND ILLUSTRATIONS

Preface

This book has been written in response to the many requests for information about humpback whales that we have received during the past ten years. A variety of books about whales and dolphins have been published during the last decade, prompted by an ever-increasing public awareness of the fragility of our marine resources. None of these, however, seem to suit the needs of those with a special interest in the humpback whales of Hawaii. Books currently available seem either too general, or they concentrate on topics too specialized for the layperson. Often they are field guides that provide isolated facts about species that most of us will never see. We have been approached on many occasions for information, both written and photographic, about the life of humpback whales: why they come to Hawaii, what they do while they are here, where they can be seen, the most effective ways to observe them, and most importantly, if they are recovering from previous exploitation. This book is intended to provide that information, and in so doing, to share with the reader our fascination with humpback whales, and the excitement we have experienced studying them in the warm, clear waters of Hawaii.

Humpback whales have been a focus of scientific study in Hawaii since 1975. We have been a part of this adventure, almost from its beginning. The time has come to make available to others what we have learned through our own field studies, our interactions with colleagues, and our study of historically important and currently popular theories of the biology and behavior of the great whales. We believe this product of our efforts is unique in providing the opportunity to learn about one species of whale in sufficient degree to recognize its behaviors and displays, and perhaps even to interpret the significance of many of them. We hope the knowledge this book imparts will make whalewatching an exciting and educational opportunity.

It is our intent, however, that this book serve as much more than a whale-watching guide. For those who may never visit Hawaii, or who may never see a humpback in its ocean home, we have tried to compile an informative and richly illustrated description of the humback whale and its behavior. In short, this book has been written for a large but select audience: those who, like us, harbor a special fascination for this knobby-headed creature with the haunting song and artful aerobatics, the humpback whale.

ACKNOWLEDGEMENTS

We recognize the contributions of many in the making of observations and the development of the ideas found on the following pages. To those who have helped us learn about the humpback whales, and who have encouraged us in our research efforts, we hope this book will convince you that the help and encouragement were well-placed.

For opportunities to study and learn about whales we wish to particularly acknowledge the contributions of Louis M. Herman. For sharing their ideas and encouraging ours we would also thank Graham Chittleborough, William Dawbin, Masaharu Nishiwaki, Kenneth Norris, Roger Payne, and Howard Winn. For long hours of constructive consideration of ideas, we thank our many colleagues in the field, most especially Ron Antinoja, C. Scott Baker, Gordon Bauer, Howard Brancel, Susan Clark, G. di Sciara, Carol Hart, Kitch Heideman, Kristi Kaufman, Joseph Mobley, Robert Slade, Mari Smultea, Helen Sneath, Peter Tyack, Randall Wells, and Kevin Wood. For helpful comments on the manuscript we thank C. Scott Baker, Alan Baldridge, Judith Ellis, Lili Hagen, Peter Jenkins, Stephanie Jenkins, Dawn Littleton, Kathy Mardon, Robert Slade, Mari Smultea, Helen Sneath, Rick Wirtz, and Kevin Wood.

Support for our research over the years was supplied by the Pacific Whale Foundation, the Kewalo Basin Marine Mammal Laboratory, the American Cetacean Society, the Animal Protection Institute, the Animal Welfare Institute, Apple Computer Corporation, Epson Computer Corporation, Walter Becker, the Coast Gallery, Center for Environmental Education, the Connecticut Cetacean Society, Contemporary Catalog Concepts, Muffin Spencer-Devlin, Richard Ellis, the Evjue Foundation, Fisher Scientific Company, Roman Hubbell, the Institute for Delphinid Research, the International Fund for Animal Welfare, Lady Ann Cruises, the Marine Mammal Commission, Burgess Meredith, the Natural Sciences and Engineering Research Council of Canada, Robert L. Nelson, Neutrogena Corporation, Ocean Activities Center, Project Jonah New Zealand, Project Jonah Queensland, Sea Grant Hawaii, Seabird Cruises, the Stern Fund, Trademark Tours, the University of Hawaii Marine Options Program, Wailea Development Company, and Windjammer Maui.

Introduction

The explosion of interest in whales and dolphins since the mid-1970s has been a remarkable phenomenon—one for which conservationists can feel justifiably proud. The transition from whale-killing to whale-watching has pricked the consciences of nations around the world. A concern for and interest in the welfare of whales and dolphins has joined people from all corners of the earth in a common front that transcends culture, race and politics.

The movement to save the whales just might become the greatest conservation success story of the twentieth century. The measure of that success will be determined by the results of research projects currently being carried out around the globe, in an attempt to gauge the present status of the stocks of whales and dolphins. Scientists are working in all the world's oceans to develop new techniques and more reliable statistical models to estimate the numbers of each of the known species of whales and dolphins.

Before the 1970s, most of what was known about these species came from the observations of biologists working on-board whaling ships, or at the shore-based whaling stations that once dotted the coasts of many nations. Working conditions were far from pleasant. Whalers operated on the basis of speed and efficiency: money could only be made if the biggest whales were caught and processed in the shortest time possible. Many biologists' reports describe the difficulties of recording the lengths of various body parts, of obtaining samples to weigh and measure or observe under a microscope, of counting and describing features of one kind or another, all the while chasing a whale carcass across the flensing (cutting) deck as it was being quickly processed by the crew. Biologists had to be fast of foot and keen of eye to collect data without getting caught in winch lines, or ending up in the rendering tanks themselves. While much was learned about the biology of dead whales through this work, little reliable information was obtained about the behavior of live ones.

Starting in the late 1950s, and throughout the 'sixties and 'seventies, a small number of scientists began studying the behavior of live marine mammals, both in the open ocean and in oceanaria, where smaller whales and dolphins could be maintained for extended periods. As the scientists studied these animals, the public flocked to the oceanaria to view these intriguing creatures. No longer were whales and dolphins seen as beasts of the ocean, meant only to serve the needs of humans. More and more, the beauty, complexity, and intelligence of these animals drew the attention of all who saw them.

In response to the increasing sensitivity of both the scientific community and the public to the plight of marine mammals, new techniques for studing them were developed. Hydrophones (underwater microphones) and cameras have displaced the harpoon and rendering tank. Where once biologists accompanied huge ocean-going whaling factories to the polar seas, researchers now set out in small sailing yachts and fragile inflatable outboard boats to view these living animals close at hand. New techniques—for identifying whales and their sex, for recording and classifying their sounds and behaviors, for assessing their population status and movement patterns, and for studying their social patterns and interactions—all of these and many more have been developed and improved during recent years.

None of the new techniques require that the subjects of the study be dead upon the slipway of a factory ship or shore-whaling station.

The research techniques in use today attempt to minimize the effect of observation on the activities of the animal under study, and have allowed us to learn more than we have ever known before about the behaviors of whales and dolphins, *as living animals.* This book takes as its focus a review of the information that has been acquired about the humpback whales using these nondestructive techniques.

Our story of the North Pacific humpback whale begins with a description of their winter home, the waters of the Hawaiian Islands. In order to place the humpback whale in its context among the other species of whales and dolphins, we outline some of the general biological characteristics of this group of marine mammals. We then describe the natural history of the humpback—characteristics of its evolution and anatomy, and the nature of its adaptations to an ocean existence. This sets the stage for a description of the behaviors in which humpback whales may be seen to engage, and a discussion of some explanations of these behaviors. The behavioral descriptions consist of a behavior "key," which briefly outlines a list of behavioral terms used by scientists studying humpback whales, and a narrative description of the contexts in which these behaviors are seen. It is our intention that, having read this material, one will be able to observe whales from shore, boat, or aircraft (further information about how to do this is provided in a later section), and determine what the whales are doing. We also describe a variety of techniques used to identify individual whales.

Following a discussion of the future management and conservation needs of the humpback population, detailed information is presented on where and how to watch for whales, the regulations which govern the activities of humans in the vicinity of whales, and what to do in the case of a stranding or observation of a whale or dolphin in distress. A brief summary of the other species of whales and dolphins found in Hawaiian waters is also presented.

Finally, we have included a bibliography of further information on humpback whales and general works on whales and dolphins for the interested reader. Throughout the text, important terms are highlighted in either italic or bold type. When a term is discussed more fully in a different section, a cross-reference is provided.

Village of Waimea, Kauai

Prologue

The Polynesian account of the Story of Earth's Creation is set down in the "Kumulipo," a sacred ancient chant. The ocean and its creatures and the land and its creatures all grew out of an initial formation of coral. Twenty-nine pairs of fish were created, each with a corresponding land plant to act as guardian. The largest of the fish was the *kohola* or whale, whose guardian on land was the *'ili-ahi,* or sandalwood tree.

The pairing of the kohola and 'ili-ahi as charge and guardian has both poetry and irony to it. The sandalwood tree, once prolific on the slopes of the Big Island of Hawaii, made its presence known by its pungent aroma, noticed even by sailors many miles offshore. Similarly, the hauntingly beautiful chorus of the humpback whale songs occurring during their sojourn in Hawaii could be heard through the hulls of visiting ships.

The sandalwood was harvested in great and uncontrolled amounts and traded for goods and currency. Years later, the humpback suffered a similar fate in the North Pacific. It is sad to note that in Hawaii today, both the kohola, and its guardian, the 'ili-ahi, are endangered species.

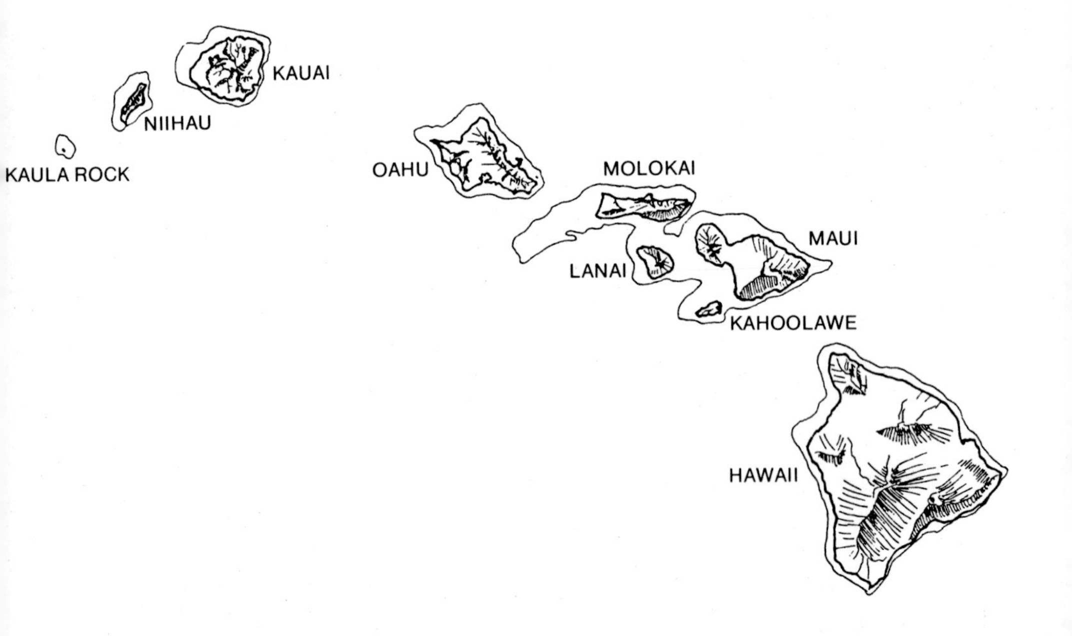

The Major Hawaiian Islands showing the 100 fathom isobath.

CHAPTER ONE

Visitors to Paradise

The Hawaiian Archipelago is a 1,600-mile long chain of over 100 small islands, shoals and reefs. The Archipelago is situated almost directly in the middle of the Pacific Basin, approximately 3,000 miles south of Alaska, and 2,400 miles west of California. The island chain has developed over 25 million years of volcanic activity in the approximate area of the Big Island of Hawaii, and has extended in a general northwesterly direction with the movement of the crustal plate on which it sits. The major inhabited islands are found in the most southerly portion of the chain, and include the islands of Kauai, Oahu, Molokai, Lanai, Maui and Hawaii. The smaller islands of Niihau, just west of Kauai, and Kahoolawe, off the southwest end of Maui, complete the area most generally referred to as the main Hawaiian Islands.

Each of the islands is surrounded by a relatively shallow underwater shelf less than 100 fathoms deep (1 fathom=6 feet). For the most part, the surrounding shelf extends only two or three miles offshore and then drops precipitously to oceanic depths of more than 2,000 fathoms. A major exception is found in the area of the 4-island group, comprised of Molokai,

The relatively shallow water extending from the leeward coast of Maui attracts humpback whales in large numbers during the winter months.

Lanai, Maui and Kahoolawe. Here the 100-fathom contour encompasses a broad, irregular shaped region including Penguin Bank extending off the southwest coast of Molokai, the Kalohi channel between Molokai and Lanai, and the Auau channel between Maui and Lanai. Penguin Bank is a 27-mile long, 10-mile wide shelf ranging in depth from 25 to 50 fathoms (see map pg. 110). It is encompassed within a major contour that drops from 30 fathoms to 300 fathoms, creating an area of upwelling that supports a major bottom-fishery.

Each year increasing numbers of visitors (approximately 5 million in the mid-1980s) flow in and out of the islands of Hawaii, drawn here by the tropical climate, white-sand beaches, and aloha spirit of Island residents. Humans are not the only regular visitors to these waters, however. In winter the Hawaiian Islands play host to a celebrity of sufficient distinction to have been designated the State Marine Mammal. While not anywhere near as numerous as the humans who come to Hawaii, the humpback whales' arrival nonetheless generates a great deal of excitement and interest. Most people who see the whales get a great deal of satisfaction and excitement from the experience, but it is clear that few really understand what a humpback whale is, and how it differs from other mammals, other inhabitants of the ocean, or other whales. In order to develop an accurate perception of the humpback whale, it is both interesting and informative to place it in the context of the general group of marine mammals known as **cetaceans.**

CHAPTER TWO

Cetaceans

Whales, dolphins, and porpoises are collectively called *Cetaceans* (Seh-tay'-shuns), after the Latin word for whale *(cetus),* which came from the Greek word for sea monster *(ketos).* Cetaceans have intrigued humans for centuries. As early as 400 B.C., Aristotle taught and wrote about whales and dolphins. In *Historia Animalia,* a book which described all the different animal forms he knew about, Aristotle wrote that whales and dolphins breathe through lungs (not gills), and bear live young (in water, not on land). He pointed out that cetaceans possess hair during part of their fetal development, that mothers nurse their young through mammary glands, and that individuals communicate underwater using sound. He even noted that the cetacean tail is positioned horizontally, and moves up and down, rather than from side to side like the vertically positioned tail of fish. Nonetheless, Aristotle chose to categorize whales and dolphins as fish, because they lived entirely in the water. Until the 17th century, taxonomists classified species primarily on the basis of the environment in which they lived.

Cetaceans are now recognized as mam-

Relative sizes of Hector's dolphin, Human, Orca, Humpback whale and the largest animal ever to live, the Blue whale.

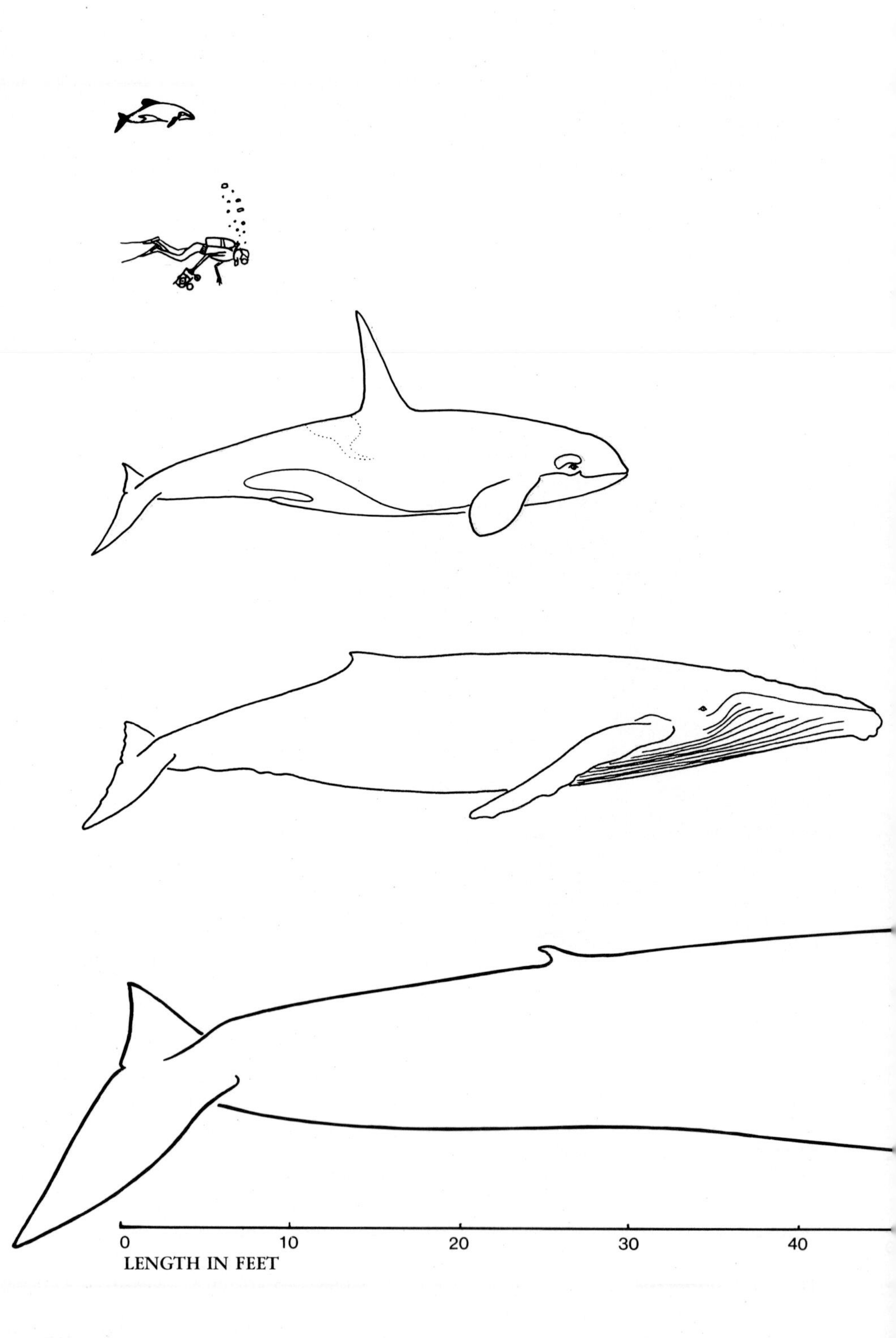

mals, one of four sub-classes of marine (ocean-living) mammals. The other three sub-classes of marine mammals are the Carnivores (which includes only the sea otter), Pinnipeds (walruses, seals and sea lions), and Sirenians (the manatees, dugongs, and the only species of marine mammal known to have been driven into extinction by humans, the Stellar's sea cow). There is not yet complete agreement on exactly how many different species of cetaceans there are. Some species have been identified only on the basis of partial skeletal remains washed up on a beach—and no authenticated field observations have ever been made.

Sometimes taxonomists do not agree whether a given species designation should be made, with arguments presented both for splitting the species off from others, and for lumping it in with an already identified classification. Consequently, we can only say that there are approximately 80 known species of whales, dolphins, and porpoises. The exact number depends on whether one is a "lumper" or a "splitter." The various species range in size from the relatively small 4-foot Hector's dolphin of New Zealand, to the largest animal ever to live, the 100-foot blue whale, found in all oceans of the world.

The bodies of whales and dolphins have undergone a great many adaptive changes to suit the demands of an aquatic environment. As they have evolved during the last 50 million years, cetaceans in general have had to face the challenge of acquiring mechanisms and behaviors that would facilitate the transition from land to sea. Intense demands were placed on finding new ways to deal with the problems of mobility, sensory perception, thermoregulation, respiration, orientation and balance, communication, nutrition, water and salt balance, avoidance of predators, courting, mating, giving birth, rearing offspring, and resting. A full accounting of the ways in which cetaceans have met these demands is not only beyond the scope of this book, but is still only incompletely understood. In this section, we will review some of the ways in which these demands have been met by whales and dolphins in general, with special emphasis on adaptive mechanisms that have evolved in humpback whales.

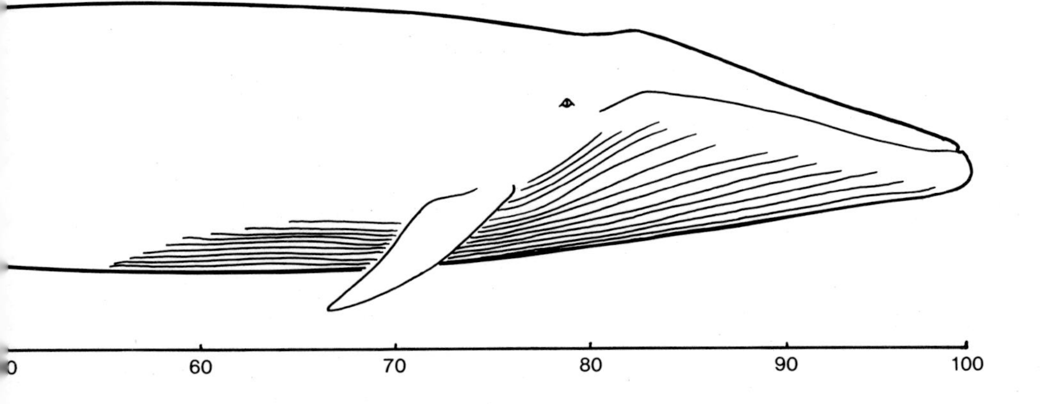

An artist's rendition of the probable appearance of *Pakicetus inachus,* the most primitive known archaeocete.

EVOLUTION AND ADAPTATION

Cetaceans have been evolving as a distinct marine mammal form since the Eocene epoch, some 50 million years ago. It was during this period that the first of three suborders of cetacea began to appear. These "old cetaceans" or *Archaeocetes* (Ar'-key-o-seats) evolved over approximately 25 million years (give or take a million or two), and then became extinct, quite likely in conjunction with catastrophic changes to the marine environment which occurred during that time.

The archaeocetes are believed to have developed from a group of hooved terrestrial herbivores (vegetation eaters) called *Condylarths* (Kon'-di-larths), a group that also gave rise to the present-day camel and hippopotamus. The most primitive known archaeocete, *Pakicetus inachus* (Pa'-key-seat-us In-ak'-us) was discovered in the Himalayan region of Pakistan, where it was deposited nearly 50 million years ago. These early cetacean species were intermediate forms which maintained some degree of structural relatedness to their terrestrial ancestry, while displaying clear modifications suited to their transition from land to water.

As they entered the rivers and estuaries in search of a more hospitable ecosystem, archaeocetes began to develop the unique anatomy that distinguished them from land animals, and defined them as cetaceans. To facilitate breathing while in the water, the nostrils literally migrated toward the top and back of the head. The neck became nearly indistinguishable from the remainder of the body, which began to elongate. The fore-limbs became paddle-shaped, the hind-limbs began to shrink, and the tail grew into a functional steering mechanism. The mouth, too, became more suited to seizing fish.

As the archaeocetes became extinct, two other sub-orders of cetacea evolved, both of which survive today. These are the *Mysticetes* (Miss'-ti-seats) or moustache-whales, and the *Odontocetes* (O-don'-tow-seats) or toothed whales. It is not clear how the three sub-orders are related. The issue is not easily resolved, because most of the cetacean fossil record is on the bottom of the ocean. Recent analysis of the chromosomes (structures within body cells in which genetic instructions are stored) of odontocetes and mysticetes support the position that they both evolved from archaeocetes. However, the morphological (body-structure) differences between the two groups (see table on page 14) suggest separate origins.

Two general characteristics of modern-day cetaceans make them immediately distinguishable from terrestrial mammals. First, the body shape of whales and dolphins is streamlined to facilitate movement through the water. This has been accomplished through the reduction of fore-limbs, the disappearance of hind-limbs, the internalization of the genitals and the mammary glands, the loss of the external ear (the pinna), and development of a fusiform (tapered at each end) profile. Second, whales and dolphins have no insulating coat of hair or fur, which further enhances movement through the water by reducing the "drag coefficient." In addition, the outer layer of the skin (the epidermis) is water absorbent. As the animal swims through the ocean, the water absorbed by the epidermis moves against the ocean water, creating an essentially frictionless interface. Further, the deeper layers of the skin (the dermis and the blubber) are rather elastic and sponge-like, compensating for increased pressure on various portions of the body under higher swimming speeds.

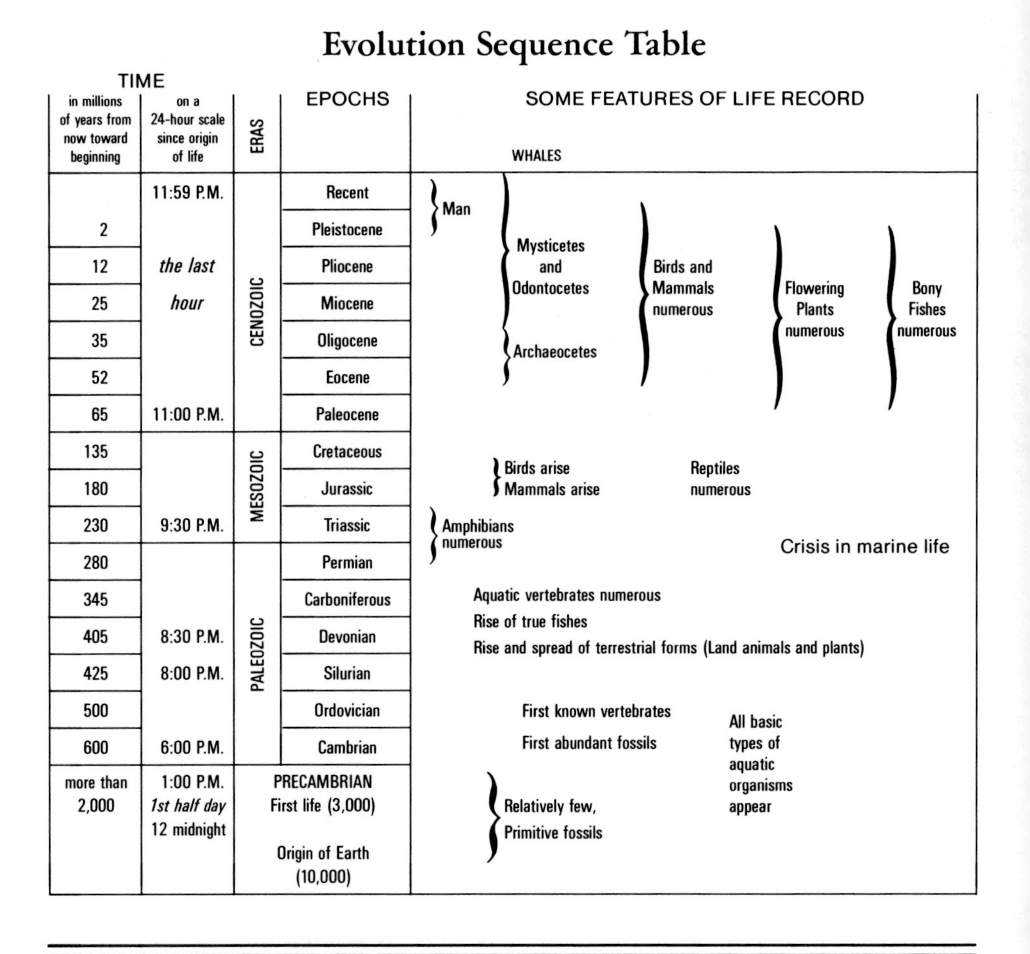

Evolution Sequence Table

TIME: in millions of years from now toward beginning	TIME: on a 24-hour scale since origin of life	ERAS	EPOCHS	SOME FEATURES OF LIFE RECORD (WHALES)	SOME FEATURES OF LIFE RECORD
	11:59 P.M.	CENOZOIC	Recent		Man
2			Pleistocene	Mysticetes and Odontocetes	Man; Birds and Mammals numerous; Flowering Plants numerous; Bony Fishes numerous
12	*the last*		Pliocene	Mysticetes and Odontocetes	Birds and Mammals numerous; Flowering Plants numerous; Bony Fishes numerous
25	*hour*		Miocene	Mysticetes and Odontocetes	Birds and Mammals numerous; Flowering Plants numerous; Bony Fishes numerous
35			Oligocene	Archaeocetes	Birds and Mammals numerous; Flowering Plants numerous; Bony Fishes numerous
52			Eocene	Archaeocetes	Birds and Mammals numerous; Flowering Plants numerous; Bony Fishes numerous
65	11:00 P.M.		Paleocene		Flowering Plants numerous; Bony Fishes numerous
135		MESOZOIC	Cretaceous		Birds arise; Reptiles numerous
180			Jurassic		Mammals arise; Reptiles numerous
230	9:30 P.M.		Triassic		Amphibians numerous
280		PALEOZOIC	Permian		Amphibians numerous; Crisis in marine life
345			Carboniferous		Aquatic vertebrates numerous
405	8:30 P.M.		Devonian		Rise of true fishes
425	8:00 P.M.		Silurian		Rise and spread of terrestrial forms (Land animals and plants)
500			Ordovician		First known vertebrates; All basic types of aquatic organisms appear
600	6:00 P.M.		Cambrian		First abundant fossils
more than 2,000	1:00 P.M. *1st half day* 12 midnight		PRECAMBRIAN First life (3,000) Origin of Earth (10,000)		Relatively few, Primitive fossils

Morphological differences between Odontocetes and Mysticetes

	ODONTOCETES	MYSTICETES
1.	use teeth for feeding	use baleen for feeding
2.	one blowhole opening	two blowhole openings
3.	skull shaped asymmetrically	skull shaped symmetrically
4.	no leg bones	vestigial leg bones

The present day sub-orders of cetaceans have been developing for approximately 30 million years. As already indicated, these two sub-orders include whales with teeth and whales without. The toothed whales are called Odontocetes after the Latin word for tooth. There are approximately 70 different species of toothed whales, with anywhere from 1 to 260 teeth found in any given species. Most of the odontocetes feed on small fish and squid, although the killer whale (pg. 144) also preys on other marine mammals, including seals, sea lions, dolphins and even the larger whales like the blue whale.

The toothed whales include the sperm whale (Physeteridae: see pg. 142) the river dolphins (Platanistidae; none are found in Hawaii), the oceanic dolphins (Delphinidae; see pg. 144), the smaller true porpoises (Phocoenidae; none are found in Hawaii), the beaked whales (Ziphiidae; see pg. 149), the belukha or white whale, and the tusked narwhal (Monodontidae; neither are found in Hawaii).

In the odontocete group, the largest whale is the sperm whale (pg. 142), about 55 feet long. There are a number of odontocete species in the size range of 15 - 30 feet which are called whales. These are found especially among the Delphinidae (including the killer whale, the false killer whale, and the pilot whale, see pp. 144-145) and the Ziphiidae, which include the bottlenose whale (very different from the bottlenose dolphin in shape, size and habit), and a number of beaked whale species (see pg. 149).

There is often confusion generated by consideration of the difference between a whale, a dolphin and a porpoise. Very simply stated, it is primarily a question of size—whales are REALLY big, dolphins are PRETTY big, and porpoises are not so big. The distinction between a dolphin and a porpoise is a bit trickier to understand, because there are both scientific and common uses of the terms. Scientifically, true porpoises are one of the species in the family Phocoenidae. These relatively small (5 - 8 foot) cetaceans are characterized by a somewhat rounded, blunt head without the protruding rostrum or beak of a dolphin. In addition, porpoise teeth are spade-shaped, while dolphin teeth are conical. Porpoises also tend to have triangular dorsal fins, while dolphins are recurved. While there is a distinct porpoise family, the use of the word is often applied by the lay person according to local custom. For example, in Hawaii, almost all local fishermen refer to dolphins as porpoises. This is also true in Florida, where the word dolphin refers to the species of fish that is called *mahimahi* in Hawaii.

Mysticete whales like the humpback

The formidable teeth of a false killer whale mark this species as a true odontocete.

have no teeth in the adult stage. (During fetal development tooth buds form, but these never erupt.) Instead they have hundreds of rather rigid strips of material, called baleen, hanging down from the upper jaw, all around the inside edge of the mouth. These strips of baleen are made of material similar to human fingernails. Roughly 30 - 40 hair-like strips of baleen grow out of indentations in the mouth, and fuse together to form wider plates. On the inside of the mouth, the ends of the baleen remain bristly and frayed—rather like split ends of hair, only much more coarse. The frayed edges of adjacent plates of baleen intertwine, forming a filtering system which traps small fish or other marine organisms inside the whale's mouth when it lets water flow in through the front of the mouth and out through the sides. The different species of baleen whales have different lengths of baleen, and different numbers of baleen plates, depending on their size and their primary food source. In general, the number of plates ranges between 600 and 800, and the length of individual plates may range from 1.5 feet to 12 feet. The baleen is much shorter in the front of the mouth, and increases in length along each side, toward the back.

Baleen whales are generally separated into three groups or families. These are the *Balaenidae* (Bay-lin'-ee-day), the *Balaenopteridae* (Bay-lin-op'-tare-ee-day), and the *Eschrichtiidae* (Esh-rick'-tee-day). We find that the easiest way to differentiate these families is on the basis of their feeding structures and habits.

The Balaenidae are comprised of three species—the *bowhead* whale, which is found only in the northern hemisphere, the *right* whale (pg. 142) which is found in all oceans of the world, and a little-known species called the *pygmy right* whale. These whales

A variety of euphausiids including krill *(Euphausia superba)* constitute an important food source for many baleen species including humpback whales.

are all characterized by a rotund figure with a large, deep mouth. These "bucket mouth" whales move slowly, are found relatively close to shore, and float when dead. Consequently, they were considered the "right" whales to hunt by early whalers, and were the first species to be brought perilously close to extinction. The Balaenidae feed on a small shrimp-like species of marine organism called krill. Krill are found in polar seas during the summer months, when they hatch and grow at an explosive rate, creating huge clouds of krill on which the "bucket mouth" whales feed. Their manner of feeding has been described as **skimming,** as they slowly swim back and forth through the swarms of krill, filtering the tiny organisms from the vast amounts of ocean water that fills their mouths. With the exception of the pygmy right whale, Balaenidae do not have dorsal fins.

The Balaenopteridae include six species—*blue, fin, sei* (Say'), *humpback, Bryde's* (Broo'-dis), and *minke* (Mink'-ee) (see appendix A,

The deep diving sperm whale is the largest of the toothed whales. Adult males may reach lengths of 60 feet.

Baleen whales differ widely in body shape and behaviors. The feeding Bryde's whale (upper right) is much smaller and more streamlined than the more rotund right whale (lower left). Note the pinkish coloration between the pleats of the Bryde's whale, one of the rorqual species.

pg. 139). All are characterized by the possession of a dorsal fin (the group of whales is sometimes referred to as "finners" for this reason, although the name is also applied by some strictly to the fin whale), a torpedo-shaped, relatively stream-lined body, and a series of folds or pleats that run from the mouth down to the umbilicus (navel). These pleats allow the whale to remain streamlined when swimming over long distances. When it comes time to feed, the whale, allowing the pleats to expand, is able to increase its mouth size by more than three times—vastly increasing the amount of water it can engulf and filter. Because of their manner of feeding these whales are referred to as **gulpers** (see Feeding, pg. 50). When the pleated whales expand their mouths this way, one can often see areas of pink coloration between the pleats. This is due to the absence of blubber and skin pigmentation, which allows the coloration of the blood just beneath the skin to show through. The Norwegians called these whales *Rorquals* (Ror'-kwal) which means, roughly, "red whales" because of the distinct coloration. With the exception of the humpback whale, all the rorquals look quite similar although they differ greatly in size.

The humpback is very different in looks and habit from the other rorquals. It has much longer pectoral fins, a more rotund body shape, wart-like bumps on its head, and an irregularly-shaped dorsal fin. Consequently, the humpback is considered to be a separate sub-family from the other rorquals.

There is only one species of whale in the family of Eschrichtiidae, the *gray* whale, well-known for its long travels up and down the coast of California. The gray whale is distinctly different from the whales in the other two families described. Rather than feeding on krill or small schooling fish, the gray feeds largely on crustaceans which it stirs up from mud and silt on the shallow ocean floor. It therefore needs neither the expandable mouth of the migrating Balaenopteridae, nor the bucket mouth of the slow-moving Balaenidae. The gray is a streamlined whale like the rorquals, but without expandable pleats or a dorsal fin. While there are two to four short throat grooves located on the underside of the jaw, these do not appear to be used to increase the mouth size during feeding. Essentially the gray whale is thought of as a **sucker.** Using its tongue as a piston, it creates sufficient vacuum to forcefully suck food out of the mud, through the baleen, and into its mouth.

The three general types of baleen whales use widely different feeding strategies (skimming, gulping, and sucking) as we have described. Nonetheless all three strategies permit individuals to feed effectively on their own. This is quite different from most of the odontocete species which usually feed in highly coordinated social aggregations. With the exception of the sperm whale and perhaps one or two species of the river dolphins, odontocetes encircle or herd their prey as a group in order to enhance the amount of food available to each individual. These differences in feeding strategy are reflected in the nature of the social groupings formed by the different species. Odontocetes in general form much larger groups which are stable over relatively long periods of time than is true of the mysticetes. Groups of oceanic dolphins may number in the tens of thousands, while it is uncommon to see humpbacks in groups larger than 4 or 5.

CHAPTER THREE

External Anatomy

The humpback whale is the fifth largest of the great whales. Its scientific name, *Megaptera novaeangliae,* is derived from its general appearance both physically and geographically. *Megaptera* means "big-winged" which refers to the humpback's long pectoral fins. *Novaeangliae* refers to the New England coastal waters where humpbacks were once found in abundance.

Humpbacks display **reverse sexual dimorphism** in size (females are larger than males in the adult stage). North Pacific females reach 45 feet and males 43 feet in length (sizes range from 36 to 52 feet). The largest recorded humpback was an *88 foot* female caught in the near-shore waters of Bermuda in the Caribbean. A mature humpback may weigh up to a ton per foot, or nearly 40 tons when fully mature. Calves range in size from 10 to 16 feet, and average 1.5 tons (3,000 pounds) at birth.

When viewing a humpback whale for the first time, many whalewatchers are surprised by its striking and unusual appearance. The head of a humpback is large in proportion to its body. It comprises nearly one-third the whale's entire body mass. The mouthline runs high along the entire length of the head dropping sharply just before the eyes. The eyes are located one on either side of the head. Each eye is about the size of a large orange, and is found just above the end of the mouthline. They bulge slightly from the orbital cavity, and are generally brown in color with a kidney-shaped pupil. Rarely do whalewatchers get a look at the

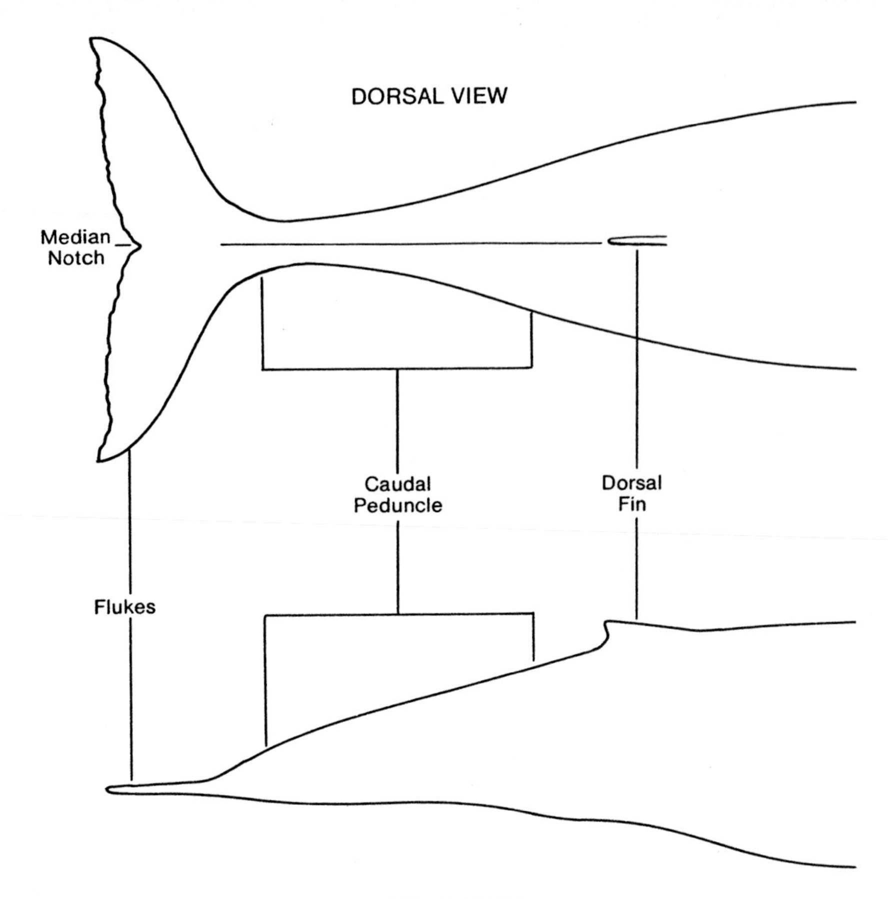

External anatomy of humpback whale (after Bennett)

Some General Terms

1. **DORSAL SURFACE:** Refers to the upper half of the whale's body along the logitudinal axis from head to tail—that part of the whale normally seen when it surfaces to breathe, exposing the back and dorsal fin.

2. **VENTRAL SURFACE:** Refers to the lower half of the whale's body along its longitudinal axis from head to tail. The humpback whale's ventral grooves, umbilicus, genital and mammary slits, and anus are all located along the ventral surface.

3. **ROSTRAL ASPECT:** Refers to forward extension of the whale's head, particularly from the eyes to the tip of the mouth, or rostrum.

4. **CAUDAL ASPECT:** Refers to the rear body portion especially the "caudal peduncle," or tail stock, which extends from just behind the dorsal fin back to the tail. This area is also referred to as the "small" of the back, while the tail was sometimes called the "caudal fin" by whalers.

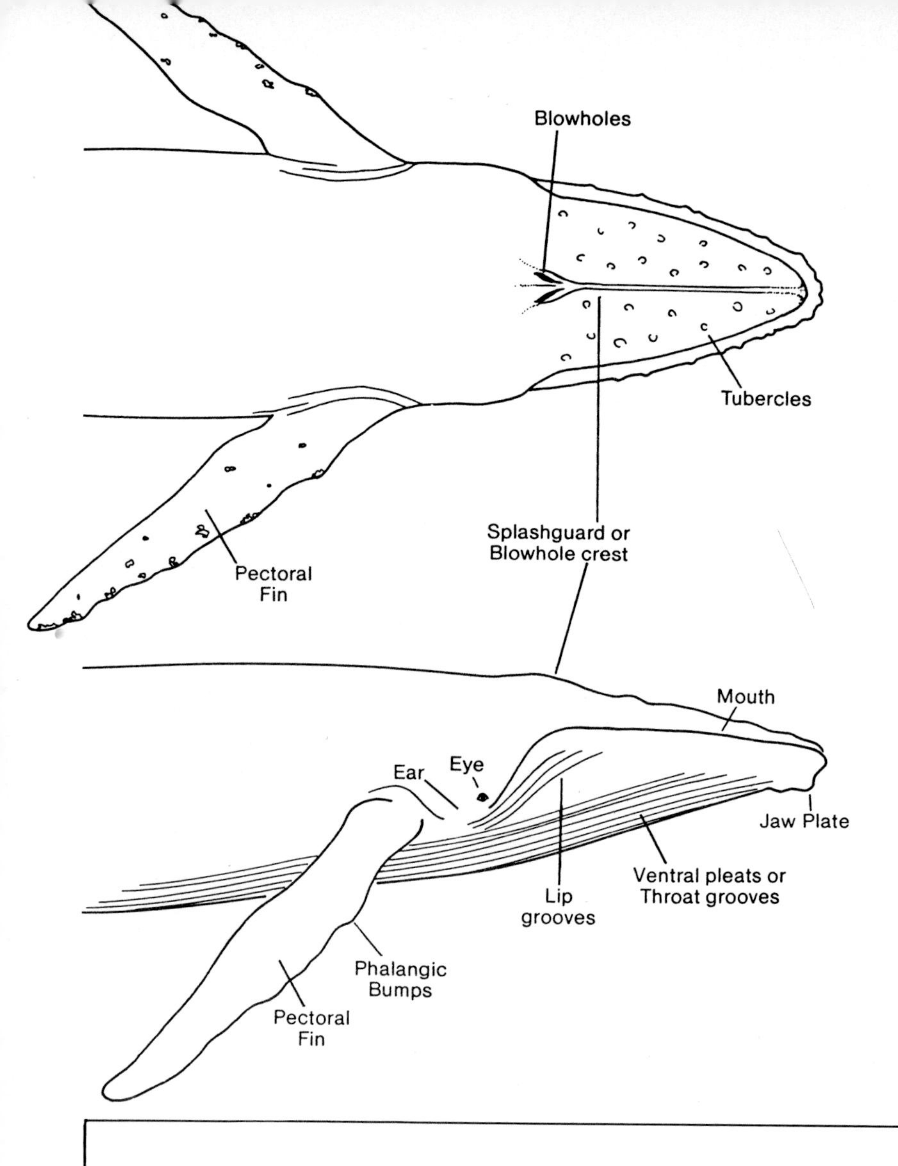

5. **POD:** A term used to describe whales which appear to be in close proximity to one another (i.e., within two or three body lengths), and apparently engaged in related behaviors (usually respiratory synchrony). A "pod" may also refer to a single whale. Use of the term is, of course, from the human observer's perspective. We do not know for certain what constitutes a coherent group from the humpback whale's point of view.

6. **INVERTED:** Cetaceans are normally considered "right side up" when their dorsal surface is uppermost. On many occasions, however, humpbacks engage in a number of behaviors with their ventral surface uppermost, or inverted.

7. **LATERAL:** Refers to either the right or left side of the whale.

Humpback whales frequently expose their eye above the surface of the water.

front of the blowholes is called the **splashguard** or blowhole crest, which prevents water from pouring into the blowholes during respiration. The splashguard also aids in locomotion by enabling the animal to expose the least amount of its body above water when breathing.

The humpback's head is adorned with curious knobs, once called "stove bolts" by the Yankee whalers. These knobs, called **tubercles** (two'-bur-kuls) or "sensory nodules," are each about the size of a golf ball. The tubercles are distributed on the humpback's upper and lower jaws and along the lips in about the same area that facial hair is found on humans. The number of

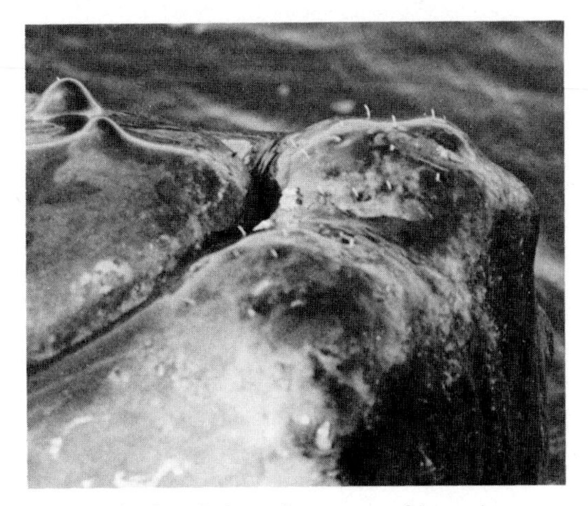

Hair can be found along the upper and lower jaw areas protruding from the tubercles.

eye of the humpback, but in occasional circumstances it does happen. In January 1980 we were conducting a benefit whalewatch out of Lahaina with over 100 people onboard the sailing catamaran Aikane II. During the whalewatch we were approached by an overly "curious" humpback which proceeded to surface near or under the stationary vessel for almost two hours. At one point the lone adult raised its head out of the water in a perpendicular position less than 10 feet from the boat. As its head cleared the water, the whale's rostrum was some 5 feet above the deck of the vessel, allowing all the whalewatchers onboard a chance to look into the eye of a whale. In this instance it is unclear who was watching whom!

The **ear** of a humpback is located just behind and below the eye. The absence of an external ear flap makes it nearly impossible to detect the tiny half-inch ear slit. The nares, or **blowholes,** are located near the center of the head, and slightly posterior to the eyes. The elevated area in

The elevated area in front of the blowholes, the splashguard, prevents water from entering the respiratory tract.

tubercles varies from whale to whale, with each possessing a unique tubercle pattern. Each tubercle contains a hair follicle, sometimes with a single light gray "vibrissa" about 0.5 to 1.05 inches long. Recent research has found that each hair follicle is connected to a nerve and has a well-developed blood supply. This suggests they may function as a sensory organ, but their exact function is unknown. They may be used in courtship activity, help detect the presence of prey in "blind spots" during feeding, or aid in navigation by detecting current and temperature changes. While in Hawaii the tubercles of highly active and aggressive whales (thought to be males) are often observed worn raw and bleeding. The tubercles whiten following healing which helps accent their unique spatial patterns allowing for individual identification from aerial photographs.

The jaw plate is located on the tip of the ventral surface of the whale's lower jaw shown on the left side of the above photo.

Many whales possess a chin or **jaw plate,** which is an irregularly-shaped shield located mid-line on the lower jaw near the tip of the rostrum. The jaw plate appears to increase in size with age, and although its exact function is unknown, it has been hypothesized that males use the jaw plate as a weapon to displace other whales when fighting. The humpback's upper jaw is much narrower than the lower jaw, and the tip of the rostrum is quite blunt.

The humpback whale's throat grooves, or **ventral pleats,** which run from the whale's chin to its navel, are deeper and fewer in number than other rorquals. The number of pleats varies from 12 to 30, with females typically possessing more pleats than males. This may enhance the food gathering ability of the females in response to the increased demands of lactation and pregnancy. A series of short curved grooves, called **lip grooves,** extend from the corner of the mouth to the pectoral fin, and sometimes just beyond. The lip grooves are asymmetrical, with up to six grooves found on either side of the head.

Examining the area of the body behind the head it can be noted that the humpback possesses a large, fleshy, posteriorly-placed **dorsal fin.** Dorsal fins come in a variety of shapes and sizes, and are usually not more than 12 inches in height. The exact role and function of the dorsal fin is unknown, but it probably aids the animal in maintaining horizontal and vertical integrity in the water. Some of the great whales, such as the right, bowhead, and gray, do not possess dorsal fins, indicating that the dorsal fin may not have any more adaptive function than the ear lobes of humans.

A little-described area of the humpback's body is the region to the rear of the dorsal fin that eventually gives way to the tail called the tail stock or **caudal peduncle.** It is the arching of the caudal peduncle while diving, coupled with the prominent dorsal fin, that most likely resulted in the name "hump-backed" whale, first coined by early whalers. The dorsal surface of the peduncle sometimes has a ridged bumped appearance, like a washboard. These bumps are often referred to as the "knuckles," artifacts created by the caudal vertebrae. These

The whale's dorsal fin shows most predominately during diving.

The 15-foot tail of the humpback is generally serrated along the trailing edge and displays a wide range of black and white pigmentation patterns.

become more noticeable when the animals begin to lose weight after many weeks of fasting, or perhaps when stress is placed on the skin as it expands to facilitate a pregnant mother's overall growth.

A characteristic feature that makes any whale readily identifiable is the tail fin or **flukes.** A humpback's flukes are broad and flat, usually 10 - 15 feet wide, and are capable of propelling the whale at speeds up to 20 mph. The flukes are normally serrated along the trailing edge, and deeply notched in the center. Barnacles often encrust the dorsal surface and tips of the flukes, while the ventral side of the flukes are characterized by a wide array of black and white patterns.

Very few whalewatchers ever get the opportunity to view the ventral side of a humpback. Some behaviors allow brief glimpses of the ventral region, but typically one has to view a humpback underwater to get a better idea of what is located where. The arrangement of the ventral region of the caudal peduncle is orderly and easy to understand (see diagram pg. 71). Anterior to the junction of the peduncle and the flukes is a protruding bump called the ventral keel or **carina.** Although found on all whales, the exact function of the carina is unknown. However, it may be important for hydrodynamic balance. In front of the carina lies the **anal slit** followed by the **genital opening.** In females the **mammary grooves** are located on either side of the genital opening and there is a small golf-ball-sized bump called the "bosk" or **hemispherical lobe** on the posterior edge of the genital opening. Following the bodyline towards the head from the genital opening, at about mid-line, is the **umbilicus** or what is commonly referred to as the "bellybutton" (we are not certain, but we think most humbacks are "innies" rather than "outies"). We have never observed a humpback calf with a portion of its umbilical cord still attached, suggesting that the cord is severed quite close to the umbilicus during birth.

Among the most striking features of a humpback are its flippers or **pectoral fins.** The pectoral fins of an adult are usually about one-third or more of the body length. They are scalloped on the leading edge with an average of 10 bumps protruding at the phalanges **(finger bones)** and joints. Pectoral fin shapes vary from animal to animal: short and wide, long and narrow, or deformed (e.g. blunt at the ends, half or all of the fin missing). In 1981 we observed a male sub-adult who was missing his entire left pectoral fin (we nicknamed him Leftie) resting near the bottom in about 60 feet of water off Makena, Maui. The fact that Leftie was resting is not so unusual, but his method of resting was. He remained in a stationary position by balancing himself on the bottom with his rostrum and his right pectoral fin—sort of a one-handed head stand! Several days later, underwater photographer Flip Nicklin photographed Leftie off Lahaina performing his one-handed

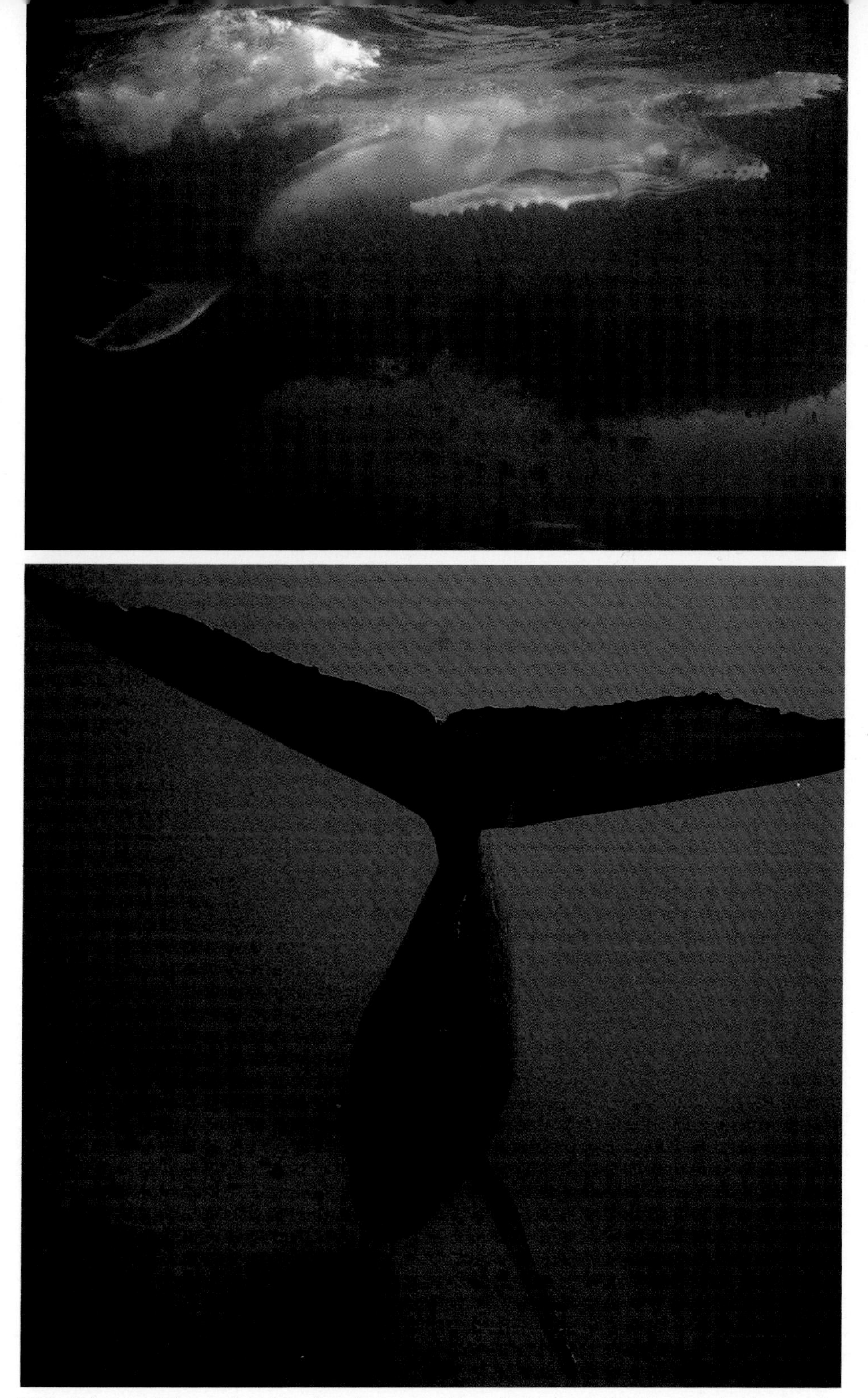

TOP: Calves are light gray in color when they are newborn, darkening gradually within the first month. BOTTOM: Leftie demonstrating his unique singing position.

The skin of whales plays host to a wide range of parasites which often leave marks like the "whale warts" seen here.

head stand once again, only this time he was singing at the same time. Besides being used as auxiliary balancing mechanisms, the pectoral fins also aid in locomotion, thermoregulation, defense, and mating.

The general skin pigmentation of a humpback varies, but it is typically dark gray to near-black dorsally and white to light-gray ventrally. A variety of coloration schemes have been observed with some animals dark brownish-gray to nearly all-white. Humpbacks in the North Pacific tend to be primarily dark, while humpbacks in the South Pacific show a higher degree of white pigmentation. We have observed humpbacks off the east coast of Australia that exhibit a remarkable range of white pigmentation on their lateral body (see photo pg. 70). In some cases the animals are nearly all-white save for what appears to be a black racing stripe down the whale's back.

The pattern of light underneath and darker on top is quite common among marine animals and is referred to as **countershading.** Countershading is useful in protecting the whales from their predators and also aids in food gathering. If you peer down into the water's depths, a dark object is difficult to detect because it absorbs light and blends into surroundings; conversely, if you are underwater and look towards the surface, a light-colored object will reflect light and be equally hard to detect, looking much like a cloud. Whale-watchers are often surprised when they observe a turquoise-blue object near surfacing whales. This is merely the white coloration of a pectoral fin or scarred dorsal fin reflecting light back towards the surface.

Calves are light gray in color when they are newborn, darkening gradually within the first month (pg. 25). They frequently have milky white patches near the tip of the rostrum and lip area. On two separate occasions, February 1978 and March 1979, all white calves were observed with their mothers south of Olowalu, Maui. It is not known if either calf was a true albino or whether the animals darkened with age since they were never observed again.

A whale's skin is well supplied with blood vessels, and where the blubber layer is not thick, some flesh-colored hues may be detected. During our research we have actually touched several humpbacks and have found the skin soft, spongy and surprisingly warm, feeling very much like a wet piece of thick foam rubber. The subdermal layer is often infested with parasitic worms which coil up into tight balls resulting in slight swellings or bumps. These **whale warts** may be found all over the body.

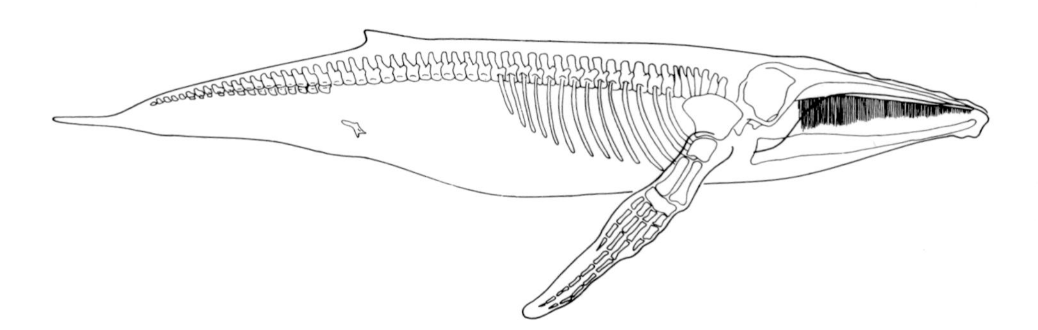

CHAPTER FOUR

Internal Anatomy

In this section, rather than describe the intricate morphological and physiological internal characteristics of a humpback whale, we will simply note major marine adaptations. In general it can be otherwise assumed that the internal anatomy of humpback whales is similar to that of large terrestrial mammals.

Surprisingly, the humpback's skeletal system comprises only 15 percent of its total body weight. In terrestrial mammals the bones comprise more than 50 percent of the total body weight. The supportive properties of sea water help maintain the integrity of the humpback's body, ridding the need for heavy bones. The bones of a humpback are only a thin shell of compact outer calcium material covering the spongy inner network of delicate webs with large spaces filled with fatty marrow. The fatty marrow accounts for nearly one-third of a humpback's body oil. This high concentration of oil makes some humpback bones float (over 80% of the fat content of the bones is found in the head), which in turn allows even the densest parts of the humpback's body to have a low specific gravity.

In general, humpbacks possess 53 vertebrae: 7 **cervical,** 14 **thoracic,** 10 **lumbar,** and 22 **caudal.** All whales lack the joint between the first and second cervical vertebrae (the **atlas** and **axis**), minimizing rotation of the head. The absence of this joint greatly aids in swimming by maintaining rigidity of the head while moving at higher speeds. The thoracic and lumbar vertebrae have a high percentage of cartilage allowing for greater elasticity and flexibility of body movement while swimming.

The caudal vertebrae are strikingly different from terrestrial mammals. These vertebrae are enlarged with extra bony processes called **chevron bones,** which provide for increased muscle attachment to aid in lifting the flukes.

The flukes of a humpback are not modified hindlimbs, but are in fact a combination of musculature, connective tissue and ligament protruding from an extended **coccyx** or tail bone. There are no bones in the flukes proper. The loss of the hindlimbs has left only the pelvis, which has been reduced to a small slender bone that is unattached to the vertebral column. This small remnant of the hindlimbs, called the **vestigial bone,** is perhaps the last lingering link the humpback has with its terrestrial ancestors. Occasionally humpbacks are observed sporting hind limbs. Whaling records from Vancouver Island, Canada, in 1949, report a harpooned humpback with 18 inch, non-functional hindlimbs protruding from its body wall.

The pectoral fins are modified forelimbs, complete with many of the bones which are present in our own arms. The forelimb has become flattened and paddle-shaped by foreshortening the **humerus, radius,** and **ulna. The humerus** attaches to the shoulder blade or **scapula,** which is a large, flat, structure providing an area for muscle attachment. There are four phalanges or **finger bones** all encased within the humpback's pectoral fins; the thumb is absent as is the case with all rorquals.

Humpbacks possess teeth only during the early stages of fetal development when a series of vestigial teeth form. The upper jaw hosts 28 small, blunt, conical teeth on each side, while 42 teeth can be found on either side of the lower jaw. The teeth are reabsorbed and disappear before birth. **Baleen** plates are present prior to birth, measuring about 1 to 2 inches in length. The number of baleen plates found inside a humpback's mouth ranges from 270 to 400 with an average of 335. Humpback baleen is deep gray or black in color with lighter, near-yellow end-bristles. The maximum length of humpback baleen is 2.5 feet, with an average width of six inches and no more than 35 bristles per plate.

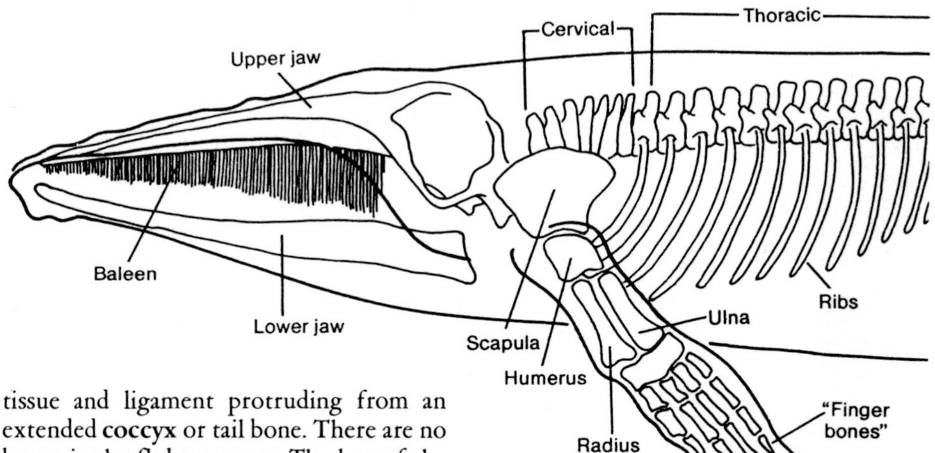

Whalers used to refer to baleen as "whalebone," and valued it for making many products. It was used to form the frames of hoop-skirts and umbrellas; as a stiffener in women's corsets; and as webbing in bed frames, chairs, and carriage seats. Alaskan eskimos split the baleen into strips and wove wicker-like baskets of incredible durability and strength.

The mouth cavity of a humpback becomes enlarged during feeding, expanding up to 15 feet wide. The **upper and lower jaws** are joined together by fibrous ligaments rather than bone. This permits the incredible gape achieved during feeding, and provides a cushioning mechanism against the stress of sudden entry of vast volumes of water. The ability of humpback whales to hyperextend their lower jaw is the result of **mandibular kinesis** in which the lower jaw becomes disconnected from the upper jaw.

The tongue of an adult humpback weighs about two tons. Although the tongue has a movable tip, it cannot protrude from the mouth as it does in other mammals. The tongue is instrumental in feeding by moving food to the esophagus (see page 52). The esophagus of a humpback is much narrower than one would expect, about the diameter of a large grapefruit. Although the humpback's throat could expand to about 10 inches, this wouldn't have been quite wide enough to have swallowed Jonah.

The tongue of an adult humpback weighs about two tons.

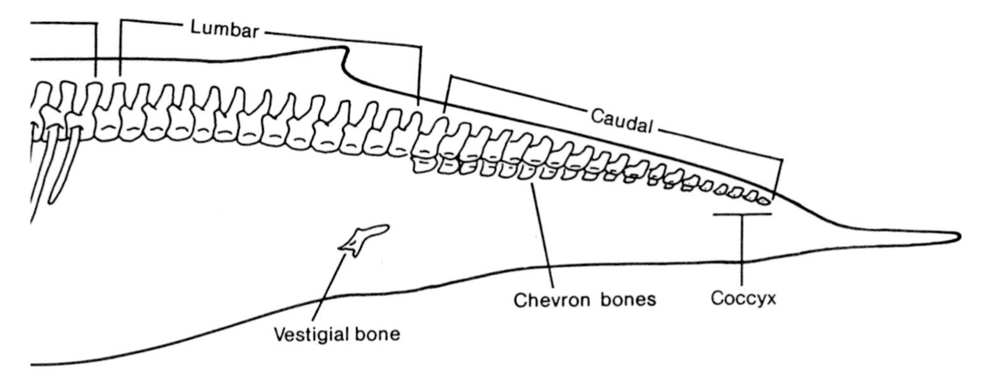

Skeleton of a humpback whale (after Bennett).

The esophagus gives way to the stomach, which is comprised of three main compartments: the **forestomach, main stomach,** and **pyloric stomach.** This probably reflects the phylogenetic connections with terrestrial ruminants such as cows, deer, and camels. Food passes from these specialized stomachs to the intestines which are about five times the body length or nearly 200 feet long.

The respiratory apparatus of the humpback whale is designed to facilitate rapid exchange of oxygen while minimizing the time spent at the surface. The blowholes lead to a short stout trachea, which can measure nearly a foot in diameter. The connection from the nares to the trachea is much more direct in whales than in terrestrial mammals. A unique system of valves prevents air from entering the mouth during exhalation, and water from entering the trachea during inhalation. Although there is no direct connection from the trachea to the mouth cavity, it is possible for a humpback to slightly dislodge its trachea enough to exhale air into the mouth. While it is unclear whether or not humpbacks have a functional olfactory capability, there are three nasal cavities located in the cartilage below the blowholes that are lined with olfactory ephithelium, suggesting that the sense of smell may exist.

Located in the barrel-shaped thoracic cavity, the lungs are relatively light but long enough to fill a stretch-Cadillac limousine. In humpbacks the lungs account for less than one percent of the body weight, compared with seven percent of overall body weight in humans. The thorax and abdomen of a humpback are very rigid, with a long, powerful ligament running just below the spinal column to assure that the spine does not sag. The humpback's rib cage is not capped with a sternum as is the case with terrestrial mammals. Instead a single bone joins just the first two ribs, allowing the rib cage to flex and accommodate increased pressures from deep dives. Consequently, one of the most serious problems that a beached humpback faces is the crushing of the lungs due to displacement of the free-floating ribs.

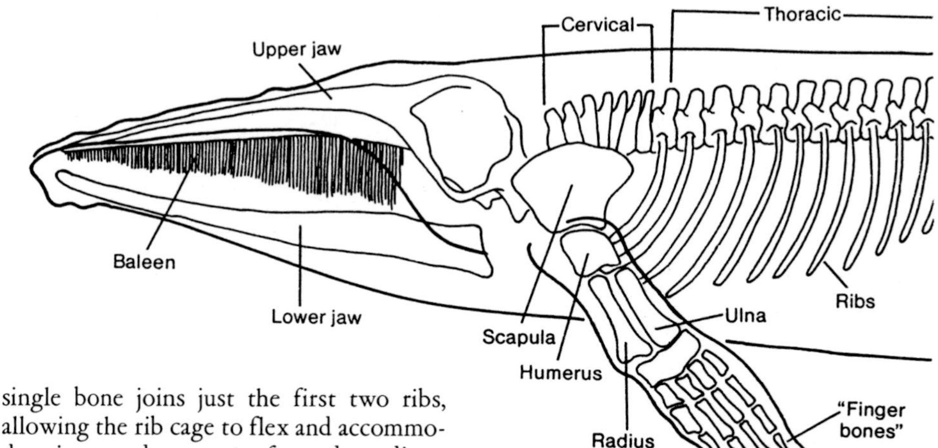

Because of the dorsal position of the lungs, and the barrel-shape of the thorax, the heart of the humpback has become much more elongated than that of most terrestrial mammals. The heart is responsible for pumping a large amount of blood: up to two or three times more blood per unit of body weight than in humans. Despite this, the humpback's heart does not appear to be any more advanced or efficient than that of terrestrial mammals. The vascular system has been modified to meet the demands of the pressures of the deep. Startlingly large veins, up to four inches in diameter, are found in the vertebral canal, while numerous, widespread vascular networks (the *rete mirabilia*) are diffused throughout the body. These networks facilitate rapid reloading of red blood cells with oxygen. Surrounded by spongy tissue, they may also serve as shock absorbers. The blood of humpbacks has a greater oxygen-carrying capacity than human blood. In addition the humpback can store oxygen in the myoglobin in its muscles. Myoglobin is a protein substance related to the oxygen-carrying hemoglobin and is responsible for the muscle's characteristic dark red color.

The humpback has the continued problem of dehydration while living amidst a sea of saltwater. Humpbacks extract water from the prey on which they feed, or from their blubber reserves during periods of fasting such as the winter breeding season. The salinity of a whale's blood and other bodily fluids is higher than that of terrestrial mammals, but is still much lower than that of sea water. Consequently, humpbacks are in danger of either ingesting too much salt from the ocean, or losing too much water. In order to maintain proper salt balance, whales have to pass large quantities of highly concentrated urine and limit all other water losses. Water loss is inhibited in part through an efficient respiratory system in which little water is lost in exhalation, by the absence of sweat glands, and by a high metabolic rate.

The kidneys of humpbacks are specialized for increased concentration of salt in the urine. They are long, flat, broad organs divided into as many as 3,000 lobes. This large number of lobes (in comparison cattle have only 25), helps remove salt from the blood stream, and provides for more concentrated urine production. The feces of humpbacks also permit additional discharge of salt from the body.

Little is known about how much or how often humpbacks excrete feces or urine. Fecal matter of adult humpbacks is rarely seen in Hawaiian waters because they fast while here. Calf fecal matter is also rarely observed in Hawaii, which is unusual since they are nursing. In 1985 we did have the opportunity to observe calf feces. The excrement was a light mustard-yellow in color, and formed thin strips about 18 inches long and two inches wide, which floated for nearly two minutes and then began to dissipate in the water.

The reproductive organs of humpbacks are located internally, enhancing the body's streamlining. The male penis is withdrawn into the genital or penile slit, located just posterior to the umbilicus. Erection of the penis is accomplished by a pair of muscles, as in cattle and horses. As the muscles relax, the penis becomes erect, and is supplemented by a sudden influx of blood. Erections in man and carnivores are accomplished primarily through an influx of blood. When the whale's penis is retracted it takes on an "S" shape. The testicles are located behind and lateral to the kidneys and above the penis. They are

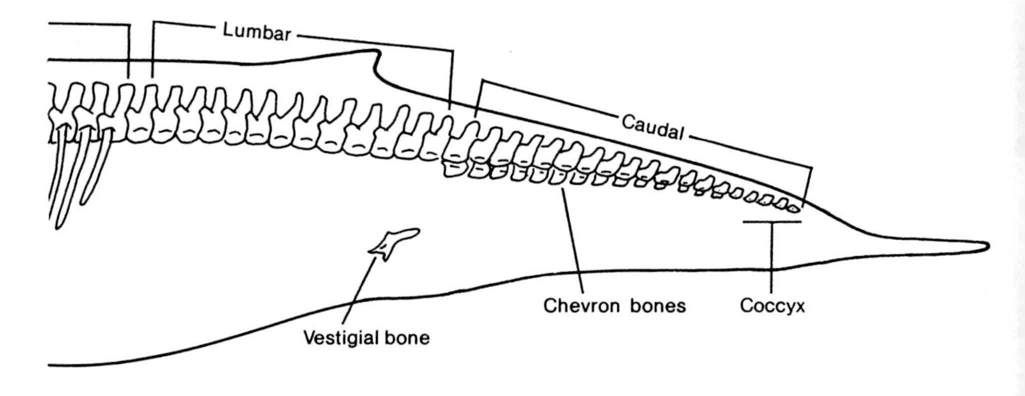

Calf fecal matter.

long, cylindrical organs which increase in size as increased sperm production takes place. Although sperm are present all year, an increased amount of semen develops in the winter months. The testes of a humpback in the winter months may weigh as much as ten pounds each.

The ovaries of the females are found in the same relative location as the testicles of males. The ovaries of immature females are smooth and flat but in the adult they resemble a bunch of grapes weighing as much as 14 pounds. Within each grape or **follicle** is a minute spot known as the **ovum** or egg. When the follicle matures it ruptures, discharging the egg into the fallopian tubes, a process known as **ovulation.** At this time the whale is ready to mate. Although rare, it is possible for two follicles to ripen and simultaneously discharge two eggs into the fallopian tubes, potentially resulting in twin fetuses should successful mating occur. However, since twin calves have never been observed in Hawaii, it must be assumed that only one fetus reaches term.

Once the egg is released, the follicle begins to increase in size, forming new tissue, which is pink in rorquals, but yellow to gray in all other mammals. The follicle at this stage is known as the *corpus luteum of ovulation.* If the egg is not fertilized, the corpus luteum begins to degenerate within 20 days of ovulation, and the pink tissue disappears leaving a white-tissued body called the *corpus albicans.* If the egg is fertilized, the corpus luteum begins producing **progestin,** a hormone which stimulates and strengthens adhesion of the egg to the uterine wall. The corpus luteum continues to function throughout pregnancy, but begins to resorb after the calf is born, until only a corpus albicans remains. In humpbacks, the corpora albicantia never disappear completely, which helps scientists to evaluate the frequency of ovulation. Unfortunately, there is no indication from corpora albicantia as to whether or not a pregnancy occurred. The humpback whale usually ovulates every two years, but one to five year cycles have also been observed in Hawaii.

CHAPTER FIVE

Breathing

Humpbacks breathe through their blowholes, with respiration functions extremely limited through the mouth. The separation of air and food passageways safeguards the animals from having water forced into their lungs when feeding. The blowholes have **nasal plugs** which remain closed until forced open by respiratory contractions. Since breathing is a voluntary act with whales, the opening of the blowholes is a measured and calculated event. Humans on the other hand, breath reflexively, in response to increased carbon dioxide in the blood.

A whale is usually first detected by the sight of its **blow,** the by-product of exhalation. When a whale inhales, it fills up its lungs to capacity each time and then exhales 90% of its air supply with each breath. Humans exhale only 25% of their lung capacity. The humpback's exhalation takes a mere half second, escaping the blowholes at over 300 mph, while inhalation takes place in a leisurely second.

Humpbacks often make a variety of airborne sounds during respiration, sometimes resembling trumpets, horns, and flatulence. Humpbacks have a characteristic high spout appearance to their blow. During our observations, however, we have observed a wide variety of types, including a double or V-shaped blow.

How the blow of a humpback is formed is debatable. It has been suggested that the blow results from the air in the lungs being under great pressure. When expelled quickly, air from the lungs cools as it comes into contact with the outside air, resulting in condensation which produces a vapor. While this may explain some of the blows created in Alaskan waters, it seems unlikely to be the case in the warm Hawaiian breeding grounds. Because of the cool air, the vapor from a humpback blow in Alaskan waters will remain suspended above the water for several minutes, while in Hawaii blow vapors are seldom observed for longer than 30 seconds.

The blow of a humpback is probably formed by a combination of water near the blowholes and water found within the respiratory tract. Humpbacks are occasionally observed allowing small amounts of water into the open blowholes after exhalation. This water is more than likely a natural part of the respiratory process similar to the residual water that is ever-present in the bottom of a skin-diver's snorkel. When the animal exhales this water is quickly atomized and sent skywards in a 20-foot high plume. Any whalewatcher downwind of a humpback when it surfaces will note that the blow is water-saturated, resulting in salt water spray on the clothing and camera lens. Since all whales can transmit viral diseases through their respirations, one should never inhale the blow (besides risking infection, the blow of some humpbacks in Hawaii reeks of four-month-old fish).

Like all mysticetes, humpbacks possess two nares or blowhole passages.

CHAPTER SIX

Swimming

The primary source of locomotion is provided by the tail or flukes. A humpback swims by moving its flukes up and down rather than from side to side, like fish. Steering is accomplished by the use of the laterally-placed pectoral fins and by bending of the body. The dorsal fin may also aid in stability, similar to a sailboat's keel. For many years it was suggested that cetaceans swim by beating their flukes in a corkscrew manner. However in the early 1960s the actual method of locomotion was established through the use of motion pictures. Forward propulsion is achieved by a powerful downstroke, while the upward stroke serves only to reposition the flukes. The ability of whales to move through the water depends on more than movements of the flukes. Buoyancy adjustments through movement of air within the body allows resting or stationary whales to exercise considerable control while surfacing. In addition to steering, the pectoral fins may be used to move both forward and backward.

Humpbacks are not fast swimmers; while able to achieve speeds of up to 20 mph for short periods of time, they average 3 - 8 mph during migration. The killer whale can move at a maximum speed of some 20 - 30 mph. The speed at which humpbacks move is highly dependent upon their activity. For example, in Alaska while feeding they move about much slower than they do in Hawaii during the breeding season. It might also be that water temperature and body weight have some effect on speed of movement. Although it may be expected that mothers and calves would move along at a rather sedentary pace, we have actually observed them swimming at speeds of 10 - 15 mph when being pursued by males. There are a number of ways in which the calf keeps pace with the mother. Ealves typically swim just above the mother's pectoral fin and to one side of her dorsal fin. This may allow them to benefit from the slipstream created by the mother. We also have observed mothers actually supporting calves on their pectoral fins or back as they swim along.

Humpbacks often leave a smooth slick area on the water's surface after slipping under (see photo below). This was once believed to result from oily deposits washed off the whale's skin as it dove. It seems clear, especially after aerial observations of diving whales, that the slick results from vortices created through water displaced with each beat of the flukes. Often a series of such slicks, referred to as the whale's **footprints** or *"puka"* (the Hawaiian word for holes), can be seen. This allows researchers and whalewatchers alike to detect where a whale has just submerged.

Underwater, the whales often seem to glide by without moving a muscle. One beat of the flukes has sufficient power to move a whale over a considerable distance. The coordinated movement of fin and fluke is keenly developed, despite the impression of early whalers that humpbacks were ungainly and cumbersome. During our underwater encounters with humpbacks we have been impressed with their ability to exercise precise control over their movements and position. Many times we have found ourselves on an apparent collision course with a curious whale. With a slight roll of the body and a tilt of the flukes the whales easily avoid us.

A smooth slick or "footprint" is left on the water's surface by vortices created with each beat of the whale's tail.

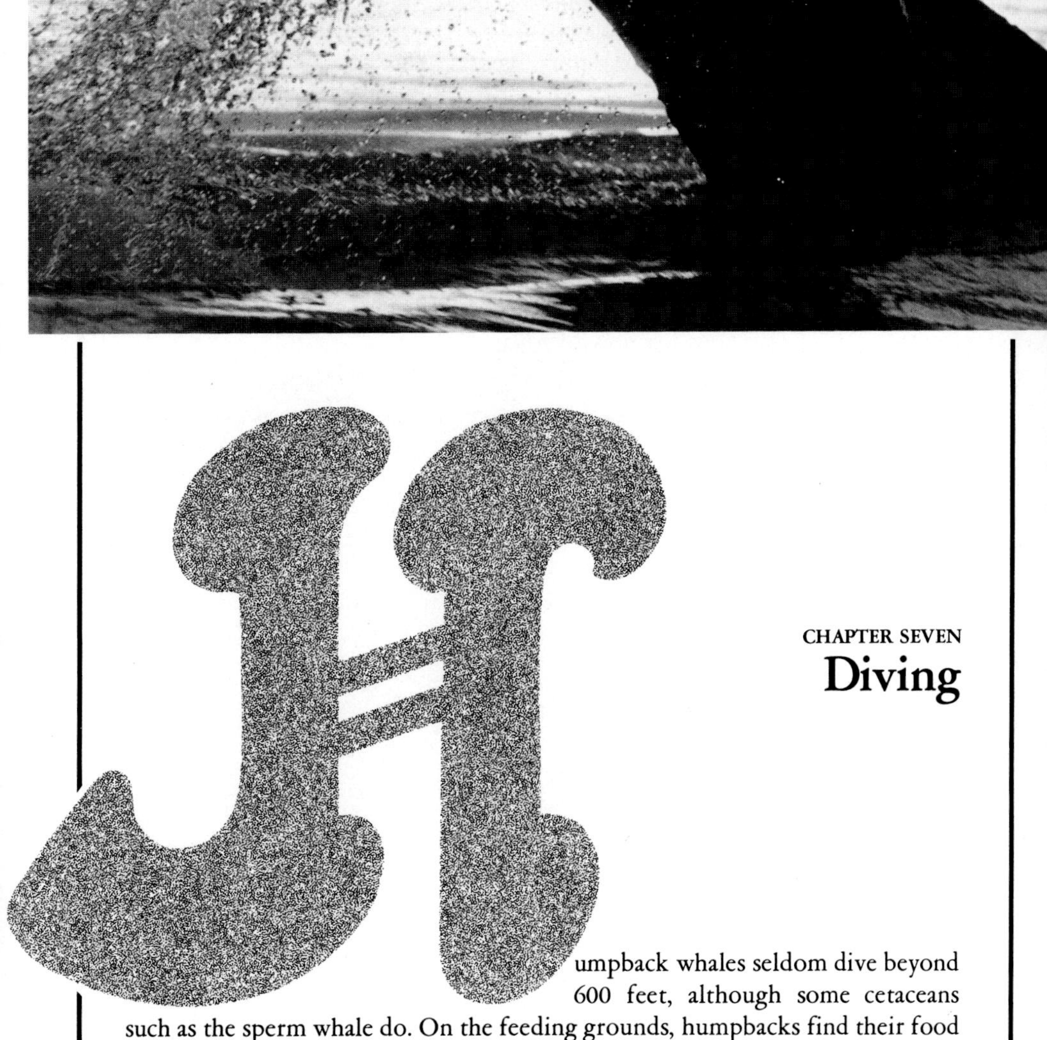

CHAPTER SEVEN

Diving

Humpback whales seldom dive beyond 600 feet, although some cetaceans such as the sperm whale do. On the feeding grounds, humpbacks find their food source near the surface so they need not dive deeply. Although they do not feed in Hawaii, we still find them within the 100 fathom (600 feet) contour. Humpbacks do not suffer from compressed air-diseases, such as the bends which can kill scuba divers, since they do not breathe compressed air when diving. Because of this they avoid the problem of absorbing high amounts of nitrogen which occurs when previously inhaled compressed air expands at the surface. When the humpback dives its lungs are compressed so that air is forced into the nasal passages, the windpipe, and air sacs around the lungs, and around the sinuses in the head. This also prevents the absorption of harmful nitrogen through the lung wall. Forty percent of the oxygen is stored in the blood which contains a high amount of oxygen storage particles called **hemoglobin.**

Although adult humpbacks have been observed to stay submerged for as long as 45 minutes, they usually stay down for no more than 10 - 15 minutes. Calves surface more often, generally every 3 - 5 minutes. Three or four breaths at the surface are usually sufficient to replace the spent oxygen. Stressed humpbacks, after being chased by other whales or boats, will often blow rapidly a number of times as though "panting." This allows them to supercharge their bodies with oxygen before diving deeply for a prolonged period.

The cold waters of Alaska place considerable demands on the whale's heat conservation capabilities.

CHAPTER EIGHT

Thermoregulation

Humpbacks must maintain a body temperature between 97° F and 99° F while contending with surface water temperatures that vary from 42° F in Alaska during the summer, to 72° F in Hawaii during the winter. Since water conducts heat nearly 30 times faster than air, swimming humpbacks must regulate their body temperature under high heat loss conditions. They do this in several ways. Because they have a low body surface to internal volume ratio they are able to conserve heat efficiently. Relative to the whale's massive internal bulk, it has little "coastline" exposed to the water because of its fusiform shape and minimal external appendages. This permits more heat to be generated by the relatively extensive internal structure than is lost through the body wall. In addition, the thick blubber layer of a humpback serves, in part, to reduce heat loss. Only a small portion of the blubber is necessary for insulation. Most of the whale's blubber reserves serve as food storage and fuel for migration.

Besides having a heat-conserving body shape, humpbacks are able to alter their metabolic rate to adjust to extensive temperature changes. Generally, because of their thick blubber, large whales maintain a lower **basal metabolism** (heat generation) rate than smaller cetaceans. However, in extreme low-temperature conditions, or when the blubber thickness becomes much reduced during the winter months in Hawaii, the metabolic rate can be raised sufficiently to keep body temperature within its critical boundaries.

Body heat is also controlled through a complex mechanism known as the **countercurrent circulatory system,** first described by a Norwegian physiologist P.F. Scholander. The circulatory system is arranged so that at the body extremities the arteries carrying warm blood from the heart spiral around veins carrying cool blood back to the heart. The exchange of heat between the two systems serves to ensure that the heat lost from warm arterial blood passes to the venous blood rather than through the skin into seawater. This system may be by-passed when the whale is overheated, permitting heat loss into the ocean.

The three layers of skin (the **outer epidermis, middle dermis,** and **inner hypodermis** or blubber), have little circulatory connection with each other. This ensures minimal heat loss through the body surface. Finally, decreased respiration rates also decrease the amount of warmth lost while breathing.

CHAPTER NINE

Sleep

Humpbacks, like the rest of us, require sleep. They can often be observed hovering just below the surface of the water, eyes closed, lying motionless save for an occasional movement of a pectoral fin or fluke. Females with calves will sometimes rest at the surface with just the blowholes exposed (sometimes causing sunburn to the back and dorsal fin and often resulting in a host of stranding phone calls by concerned whalewatchers).

Whale sleep is different than the sleep experienced by humans. A resting humpback appears to place itself in a sleep rhythm. Every fifteen minutes or so it will slowly rise to the surface, blow, and then re-submerge. Whales rely on a string of such "naps," rather than engaging in an extended period of sleep as humans do.

It has been hypothesized that whales require less sleep than humans because an aquatic environment induces a unique brain state. Some small cetaceans, such as the bottlenose dolphin, are believed to live in a continuous **alpha state**—a state of mind that humans experience when they are relaxed. Studies of humans have shown that when placed in an aquatic environment in which traditional gravitational forces are removed, the brain spends relatively more time in the alpha state and the body requires less sleep. For example, humans normally requiring eight hours sleep per day need only one hour. Whether it is appropriate to think of whales experiencing similar extended periods of alpha rhythm remains to be established. Perhaps whales sleep for only brief periods at a time because they are voluntary breathers, prohibiting extended periods of deep sleep. It may also be the case that brief sleep episodes reduce vulnerability to predation and stranding.

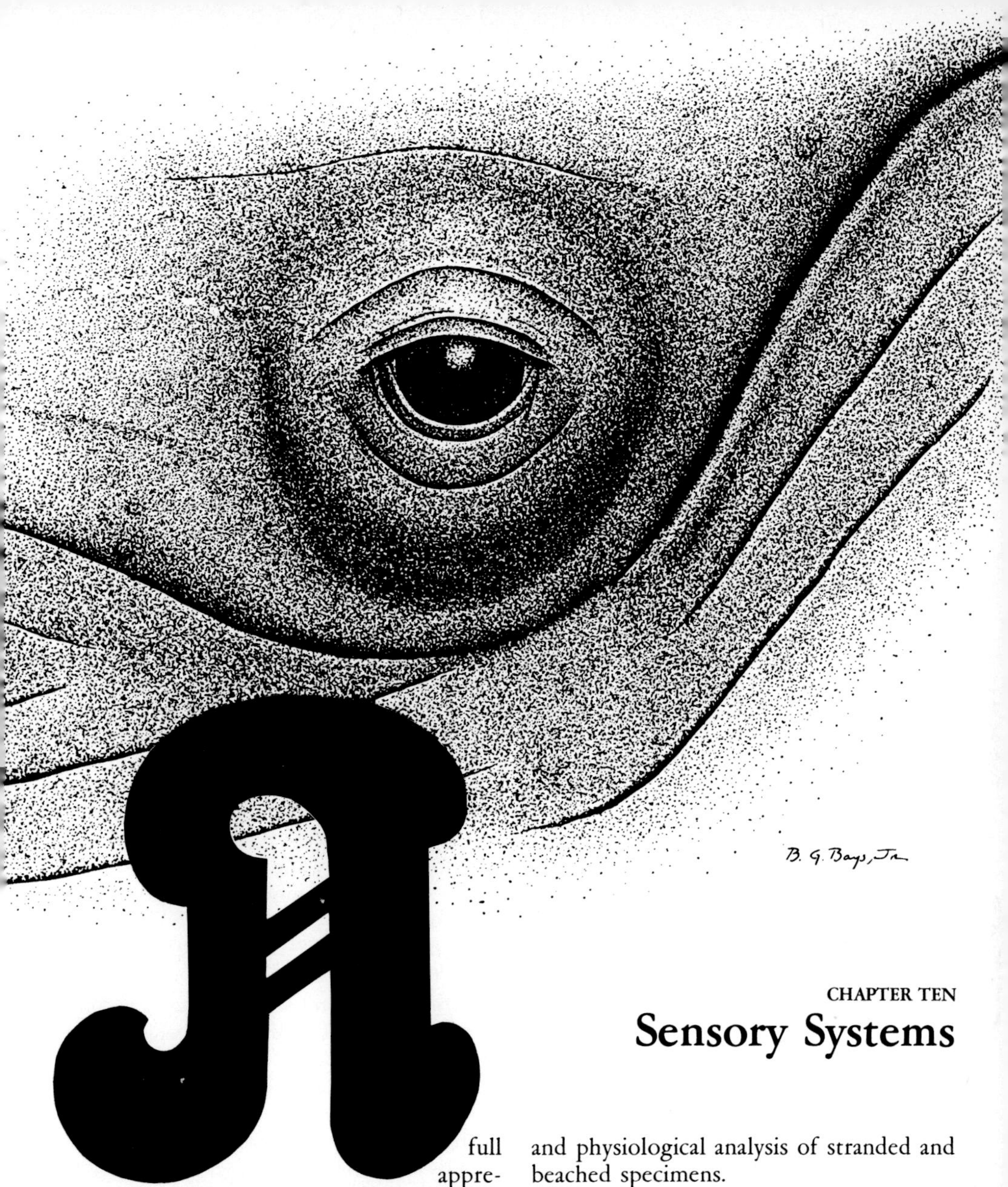

B. G. Bays, Jr.

CHAPTER TEN

Sensory Systems

A full appreciation of the sensory capabilities of a particular species depends upon controlled laboratory tests of live animals. This has never been possible with animals as large as the humpback whale. Consequently, our knowledge of the humpback's sensory capabilities is based on what has been learned from studies of smaller cetaceans maintained in laboratory settings, and inferences from field observations. In addition, descriptions of the visual system have resulted from examination of specimens recovered during whaling operations, and physiological analysis of stranded and beached specimens.

The general picture that emerges from these various observations and investigations is that humpbacks have superb **vestibular** (balance) control, keen **tactile** (touch) sensitivity, excellent **hearing,** good **vision,** a sense of **taste** in at least some areas, and probably have little (if any) **olfactory** (smell) capability.

In order for a highly mobile species to survive, it is imperative that mechanisms exist which permit long-distance interrogation of the environment, as well as an ability to detect variations at close range.

Because the density of water is approximately 800 times greater than that of air, light penetration is considerably reduced over distances of more than a few feet. On the other hand, sound transmission is much enhanced. Consequently, the auditory system is a better candidate for monitoring over long distances than the visual system. It should come as no surprise, therefore, that cetaceans have a very highly developed sense of hearing. This is reflected both in the adaptations within the ear itself, and in the elaborate development of the auditory systems within the brain.

Localization of sound sources in mammals depends upon receiving slightly different signals to the two ears: different in terms of intensity and in terms of time. While these differences are slight, they are critical. A sound that reaches both ears exactly simultaneously with equivalent intensity cannot be readily localized. In air, the two ears are isolated by the bony structure of the skull, so that off-center sounds must travel relatively further to reach one ear than the other. However, the density of biological tissue is equivalent to that of water, so that underwater the ears of terrestrial mammals are no longer isolated, and it becomes almost impossible to localize sounds. Whales and dolphins have overcome this problem by the development of elaborate foam-filled **sinus cavities** which surround the **middle** and **inner ears,** creating an air-barrier that restores localization ability. These air "cushions" also protect the ear from damage due to radical changes in pressure during deep dives. In addition, fine resolution of sound traveling through water depends upon frequencies that are some four times higher than would be necessary in air. Consequently the bones of the middle ear of marine mammals must be much heavier and more rigid than those of terrestrial mammals in order to maintain the fidelity of the higher frequencies.

Additional modifications have occurred with the **outer ear** to enhance hydrodynamic streamlining, and to prevent water from being forced under pressure against the middle ear structures. Unlike most terrestrial mammals, cetaceans have no **external pinna,** or earflap. Also, a heavy wax plug exists in the **auditory meatus** (ear canal) to keep water out.

There exists a great deal of controversy about the exact nature of the mechanisms involved in cetacean hearing, especially with regard to the role the external ear plays in relaying sound to the inner ear through the bony structures of the middle ear. Two opposing theories have generally been put forth. On the one hand, a number of researchers have argued that the external ear is relatively unimportant in sound transmission. Instead, they propose that sound pressure changes are "telegraphed" through the bones of the lower jaw and fatty deposits surrounding the middle ear. Others argue that the ear canal is as functional in marine mammals as in terrestrial mammals. Each side claims the issue has been experimentally decided in their favor. The controversy has become rather heated at times, with a recent publication suggesting that the conclusions reached by the opposing side were "based on purely intuitive or subjective observation . . . arrived at with only a rudimentary application of anatomy and none of acoustics." The resolution of the issue is rather difficult, as it is nearly impossible to carry out neuroanatomical studies on a living dolphin, and totally impractical to consider doing so on an animal the size of a humpback whale.

Regardless of the specific channel through which the sounds are received, it is clear from field observations that hearing is an important sense for humpback whales. It would be impractical to conclude that a species would have the capability to produce the elaborate vocalizations that can be heard from humpbacks without a similarly elaborate hearing system. In addition, it is apparent that humpbacks are aware of the presence of other whales and boats at considerable distances. It is extremely difficult for a swimmer to approach a whale without the whale becoming alerted. On one occasion, we approached a calf that had strayed from its mother. According to our shore-spotters, the mother was nearly a kilometer away. On our approach the calf made two or three jaw-clapping noises, which resulted in an immediate and high-speed approach by the mother, who then physically moved the calf

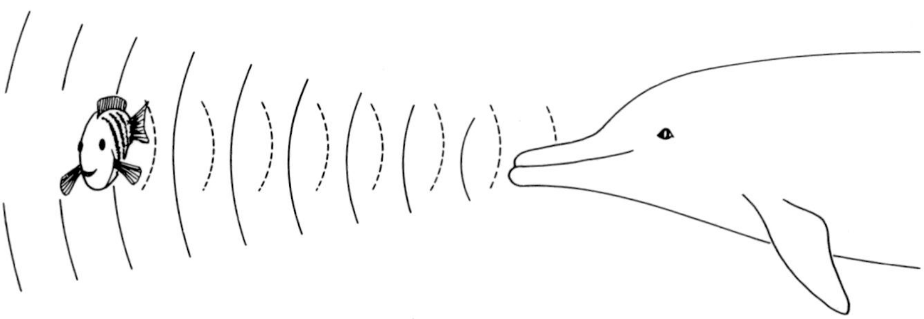

ECHOLOCATION

CERTAIN MARINE MAMMAL SPECIES have the ability to produce very high frequency sounds, which can be transmitted over relatively long distances. The sounds strike objects in the water (for example, fish, land formations, flotsam and jetsam, ocean flora, etc.). The "echo" from the sound returns to the transmitting animal, and provides information about the nature of the object. This capability is referred to as "echolocation," since the animal is able to locate objects in the water on the basis of the returning echo. It is also referred to as "biosonar," since it is a biological process similar in theory to the use of acoustic signals in sonar systems found on ships and submarines (the word SONAR is obtained from the phrase SOund NAvigation Ranging). Only odontocetes have been found to possess echolocating ability. Seals and sea lions, and two or three species of baleen whale (including humpback) have been observed in situations in which echolocation could be used to advantage, yet none of these species have shown evidence of having such an ability.

Echolocation sounds are produced in air sacs attached to the respiratory tract, and are directed through fatty deposits in the forehead (the "melon"). The sounds are produced in pulses, so that as the echo from each pulse returns, the animal is able to compare it with the outgoing pulses. The difference between the two provides the animal with information about the distance to the object, the size of the object, its shape, and even the material from which it is made. To the human ear, the echolocation pulses sound like a series of rapid clicks. This is because we can only hear a portion of the frequencies which are contained in the pulsed sounds. Echolocating abilities are not yet well understood, but it seems clear that it is a highly adaptive mechanism for quickly scanning the environment to find out what may be beyond the limits of visibility below the water's surface. Odontocetes' sonar capabilities do not operate in air.

The cetacean eye appears well adapted for both underwater and in-air vision.

some distance away. Clearly there is need for concern that ever-increasing noise generated by recreational boat traffic in the vicinity of breeding humpback whales may interfere with their social organization and mating activities.

There is a rather widespread misconception that whales and dolphins have poor eyesight. This mistaken notion is based on the expectation that an eye developed on land will be useless underwater and the assumption that vision is so restricted underwater as to be pretty much useless in any case. In fact, it appears that most species of cetaceans have quite good visual ability both underwater and in air. The cetacean eye has a number of modifications developed to handle changes in available light with varying depths, the buffeting of the eye from direct contact with the ocean and the particulate matter therein, the high salt content of sea water, the different demands of aerial and underwater vision, and the pressure changes experienced in deep diving.

The **sclera** or skin of the eye in the humpback is thick and rigid to allow it to maintain its shape under increased atmospheric pressure. The eye is surrounded by a shock absorbing system of specialized blood-engorged spongy tissue called the **rete mirabilia.** The humpback whale, like all other cetaceans (with the exception of the Ganges River dolphin) has a "fish-eye" (circular) lens that allows light to focus properly on the **retina** underwater. Such a lens is ill-suited for focusing light rays in air, but this problem has apparently been overcome by the development of an irregularly shaped **cornea** which acts like a bifocal lens, and compensates for the inability of the fish-eye to properly focus light on the retina in air. Consequently, when a whale looks at something in air, it appears to be rolling its eye back in its socket as it attempts to view through the flattened portion of the cornea. In addition, the retina is covered with a special highly reflective material called the **tapetum lucidem,** the same material that causes eyeshine in cats at night. This reflective material enhances the light-gathering characteristics of the eye and improves vision under conditions of low illumination, such as would be found with increasing depths beneath the water's surface.

Because the whale's eyes are situated one on either side of its huge head, it would appear that the visual fields of the individual eyes do not overlap. However, this is not the case. While the predominant visual field of the whale is outward to either side, there is an area below the whale's head and forward of its eyes that can be viewed stereoscopically (with both eyes). This

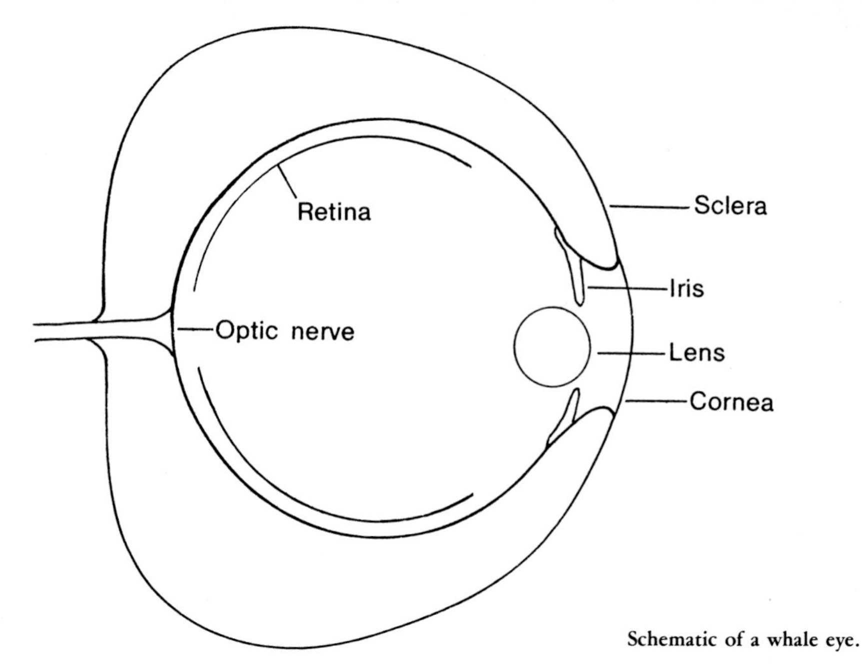

Schematic of a whale eye.

otherwise small area is enlarged by the mobility of the whale's eyes within the sockets. By bulging the eyes out by a few centimeters, the overlap in the visual field is increased. Like rabbits, humpback whales can also see somewhat behind, if the object of interest is far enough out from the midline of the body.

The cetacean eye appears to be specialized for brightness and motion detection. It does not contain color receptors, so the humpback is color-blind, with its most sensitive light detection capability in the blue range of the spectrum. Nonetheless, vision serves as an important sense in gathering information at close range. The wide variations in brightness patterns among whales facilitate individual visual identification. It may also be the case that in-air vision plays a role in migration. Changes in day-light, or the movement of celestial bodies may guide the whale over deep-ocean distances, while prominent landmarks may facilitate orientation near-shore.

There has been considerable interest developing over the last two or three years in the issue of whether or not cetaceans might derive information for location and movement from differences in the magnetic field of the earth's crust. This has necessarily been studied most often in the odontocetes, and some intriguing results have been found. There is evidence that areas where dolphins are most frequently found stranded are characterized by high levels of magnetic "noise" or anomalies. Little work has yet been done with baleen whales, and it remains questionable whether or not humpback whales detect differences in magnetic fields.

The humpback appears to have a well-developed tactile (touch) sense. There are a number of body areas that are highly sensitive, including the lips, genital area, sensory nodules, and areas of the pectoral fins. The importance of tactile stimulation is especially apparent when watching the interactions between mother and calf, and the activities of whales in apparent courtship maneuvers.

While there is little evidence that cetaceans have the ability to smell, it has been established that at least some species of odontocetes discriminate a variety of tastes. While such experiments have never been conducted on humpback whales, it is quite probable that **chemoreception** (taste sensitivity) plays a role in feeding. The distribution of a variety of baleen species in their feeding areas can be predicted on the basis of salinity patterns in the ocean associated with accumulations of zooplankton and other food resources. Taste appears to play an important part in communicating hormonal and emotional states in the odontocetes; whether any of the baleen whales have sufficient development of the taste buds to permit the same patterns of use is not known.

Humpback whales, like all cetaceans, have an exquisite sense of balance and body orientation. While they often appear clumsy and ungainly as they surface to blow, when viewed underwater they can be seen using pectoral fin and flukes to move easily and quickly in any direction, turning at a moment's notice to their side or back.

The humpback whale, like other cetaceans, is well-adapted to extract a wide range of sensory messages from its watery world, as well as from the air above it. Humpbacks have a complex and well-tuned sensory-processing system that allows them to both perceive and learn from their environment.

CHAPTER ELEVEN

Intelligence

One of the major factors that has contributed to an increased sensitivity in our interactions with whales and dolphins is the finding that they possess a large and complex brain. This has led to an expectation that cetaceans should demonstrate learning capabilities at least as rich and varied as non-human primates (monkeys and apes). Perhaps one of the most frequent questions we are asked is how "intelligent" whales are. Unfortunately, there is no direct answer to the question.

The concept of intelligence is vague. Even with reference to the human species there is little agreement on what is meant by the term. We prefer to ask how well a species is able to adapt to the changing demands of a volatile environment. In this sense, an intelligent species is one that decides what to do in the present on the basis of a complex integration of information derived in large part from past experience. Ideally, the past experiences that influence present decisions include not only what a given individual has experienced, but also what conspecifics (members of the same species) have experienced.

Viewed in this way, it can be seen that intelligence is dependent upon complex learning capabilities, abstract information-processing skills, and an intricate social communication network. The challenge is to figure out how to measure these capabilities in a 40-ton animal. Fortunately, there are solutions to the problem other than trying to find a way to keep a humpback whale in a testing tank long enough to give it an IQ test.

There are at least three lines of evidence that suggest that humpback whales do engage in complex mental processes. The first line of evidence has to do with the amount of brain matter whales have for learning and information-processing. Harry Jerison, a professor of comparative neuro-anatomy (the study of the brain structure of different species) at UCLA, has developed a method for ranking species in terms of their "thinking" power. The method is based on the assumption that, for any given body size, a minimum brain size is required in order to make that body function properly. As an analogy, one might consider that the air conditioning unit required to keep a one bedroom condominium cool is not going to be sufficient to keep a 50-story office building cool. One can, theoretically at least, take an average of the brain sizes of all the different species that have a similar body size. This should suggest the size of brain it takes to run that size of body. Any individual species that has a brain bigger than average for its body size category can be assumed to have extra brain-power available for thinking and problem solving. That amount of brain remaining once the basic requirement for that body size is removed can be used to compute an index of intelligence called the **encephalization quotient.**

When the encephalization quotients for a wide range of species are compared, Jerison finds that humans, primates, and cetaceans rank highest in the amount of brain material available for intellectual functioning. On that basis, we might expect to find that humpback whales show a wide range of learning capabilities. There is some disagreement whether relationships between body size and brain weight tell us much about intelligence. One consideration that must be kept in mind is that baleen whales are not subject to the same constraints on body size that may limit growth in terrestrial mammals and predatory ondontocetes. This might invalidate comparisons of brain/body weight measures between terrestrial mammals and baleen whales.

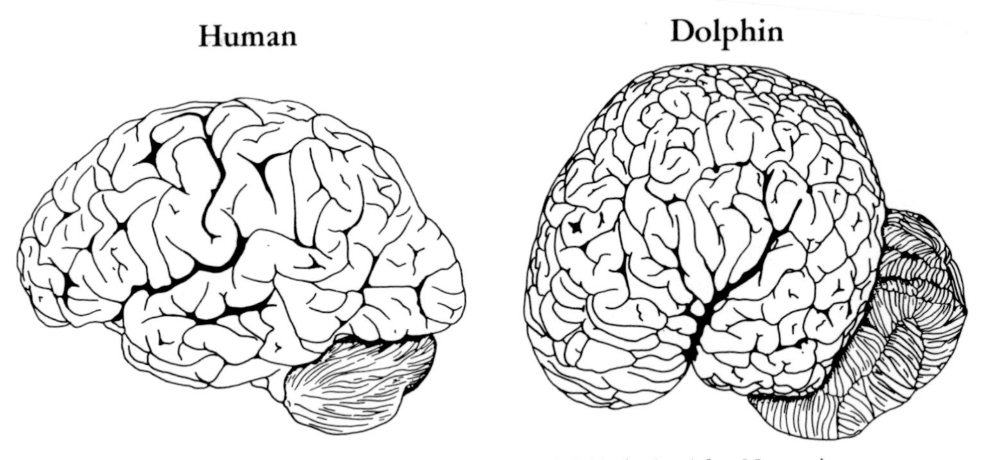

The relative size and shape of the human and bottlenose dolphin brains (after Morgane)

A second line of evidence indicating intelligence in humpback whales concerns the actual structure of the cetacean brain. Not only is the brain of the humpback whale large, it is structurally complex. Most notably, the humpback, like other cetaceans, has a richly elaborated cerebral cortex. The cortex is the outer covering of the brain, where it is believed much of the activity associated with thinking and problem-solving occurs. Although the cetacean

cortex is somewhat thinner than the cortex of humans and non-human primates, it appears to be somewhat more convoluted (folded). The general impression is that the structural complexity of the cetacean brain is quite capable of supporting abstract information processing and integration skills.

The third line of suggestion that humpback whales are capable of complex mental processes has to do with their communication skills. We discuss elsewhere (pg. 73) aspects of the communication system of the humpback whale. Rather than duplicate that discussion here, we will simply note that there is a great deal of evidence that humpback whales have the ability to signal each other for a variety of purposes. As is true of so many other aspects of cetacean behavior, we know very little of the specific meaning of the many sounds heard. Inroads are being made, however. Analyses of right whale sounds in Argentina have shown that some intriguing relationships exist between the sounds made within groups of whales and the activities in which they are engaged. Efforts to understand the sounds of humpback whales will, it is hoped, begin to meet with similar success. Attempts are currently under way to understand the meaning of a variety of social sounds emitted by humpback whales.

There seems little doubt, overall, that humpback whales are intelligent, according to our earlier definition. The feeling is strongly supported by observations of humpback whales in the field. It is very important that, as scientists, we avoid slipping into anthropomorphizing and fantasizing about the levels of "thought" and "emotions" that may be present in the whales we observe. Nonetheless, we cannot avoid developing a deep attraction for these awesome beings, as we watch them traveling along Hawaii's tropical shores looking for mates, caring for their young, learning about the responsibilities and opportunities of a maturing humpback whale, and competing vigorously for the opportunity to pass their genetic heritage on to the next generation. And, all the while the whales are here, the plaintive cry of their song seems to reach out and challenge us to work that much harder to understand the complexities of their life and needs, and strive to ensure that they will be successful in their quest to survive.

CHAPTER TWELVE

Feeding

Whales are a part of a relatively short food chain which begins with **phytoplankton** that floats in the upper layer of the sea. Phytoplankton synthesizes sunlight into energy and in turn is consumed by **zooplankton.** The zooplankton and phytoplankton are the food source for small fishes, and together these links in the chain are consumed in large quantities by the whales. The chain is completed when waste products from digestion and dead whales sink to the floor of the ocean and decompose. This decomposing matter, also known as **detritus,** is recycled as nutrients for the phytoplankton.

Humpback whales have yet to be observed feeding in Hawaii. They appear to feed only during the summer months in the food-rich waters of southeast Alaska and the colder polar waters further north. Their diet is a mix of euphausiids (krill), copepods, and small fish, primarily herring and capelin.

Mouth agape, a humpback whale bursts upward through its bubblenet. Note the leaping fish to the right of the surfacing whale.

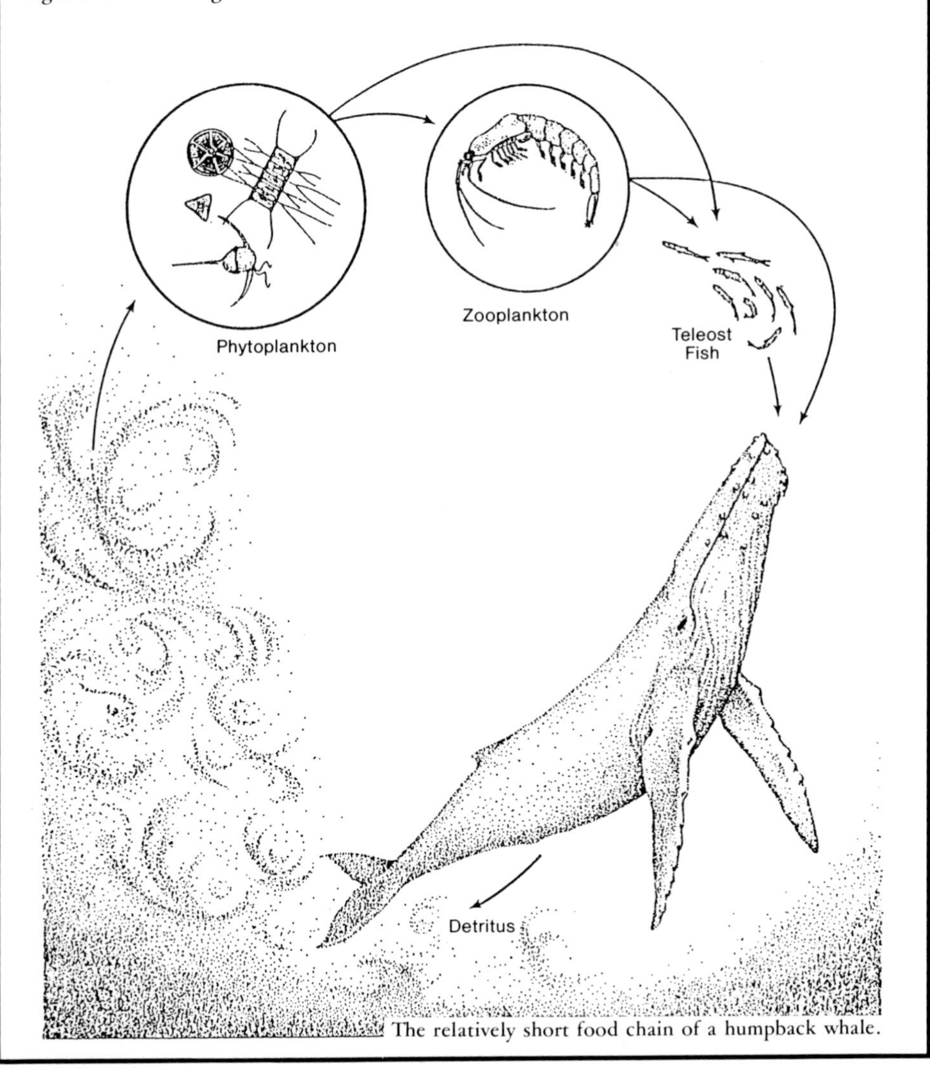

The relatively short food chain of a humpback whale.

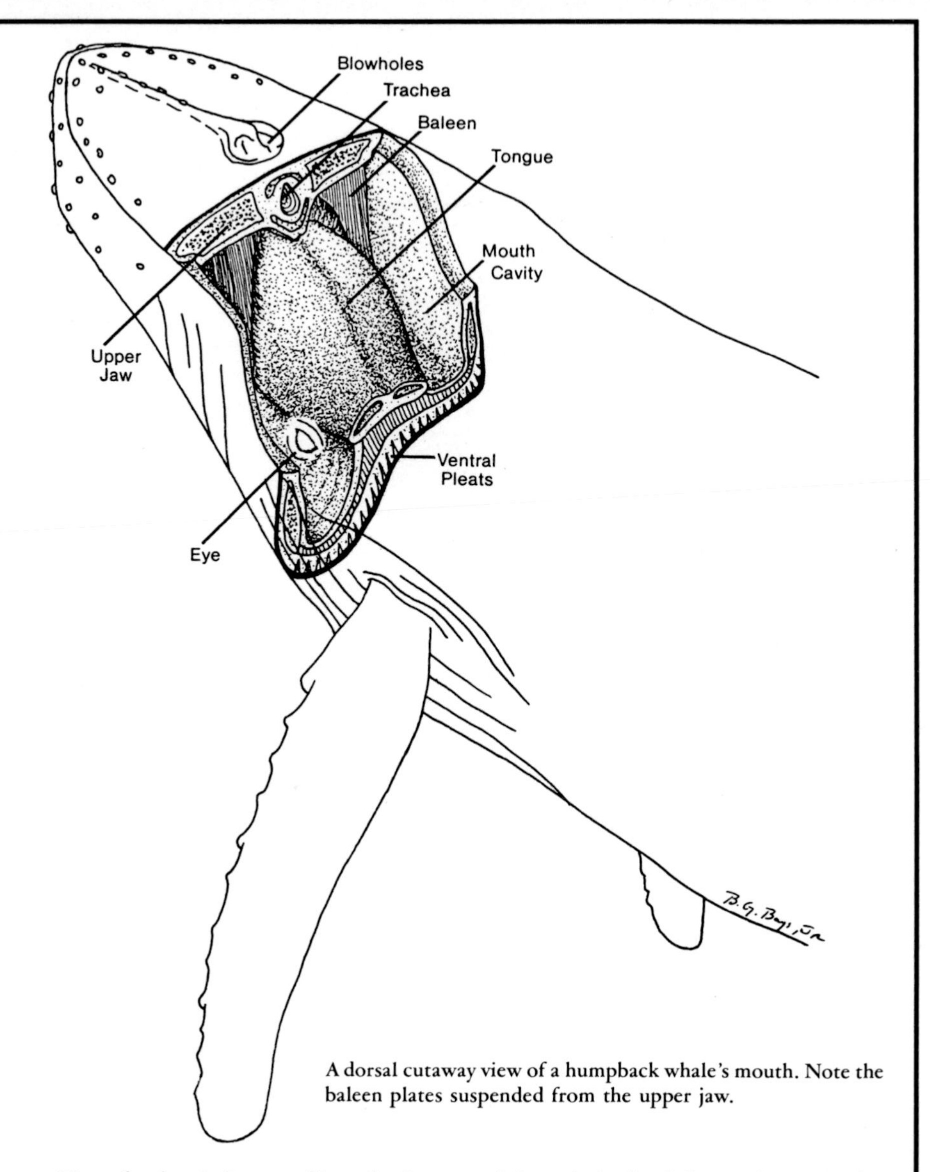

A dorsal cutaway view of a humpback whale's mouth. Note the baleen plates suspended from the upper jaw.

Humpback whales are filter feeders, straining their food from the water by means of baleen plates. As described earlier (pg. 15), baleen whales are divided into three filter feeder types: skimmers, gulpers, and suckers. Skimming whales move along slowly at the surface with their mouths wide open, through blooms of zooplankton (e.g. right and bowhead whales); gulpers take in large quantities of food, by rushing at it from the side or below (e.g., rorquals, including the humpback); and suckers create a suction action with the tongue and the palate to draw water and food into the mouth (e.g. gray whales).

The fringed interior of the humpback's baleen plates, forms a fibrous mat suspended from the roof of the mouth. The whale opens its mouth to engulf a large quantity of water. The animal then pushes its tongue upwards and drives the water through the spaces between the plates. When the food becomes trapped within the fibrous mat the tongue is drawn posteriorly, carrying the food mass toward the rear

of the mouth cavity to the throat and esophagus.

When feeding, humpbacks employ a variety of techniques which appear related to the species and density of the prey. Two feeding methods are commonly employed: **lunge feeding,** and **bubblenet feeding.** Lunge feeding appears to be used when krill, herring or capelin are abundant. When lunge feeding, the humpback swims through an aggregation of its prey, opens its mouth near the surface of the water, and engulfs the prey. Lunge feeding may occur in any of three varieties: vertical, lateral, or inverted, depending upon the orientation of the animal when it breaks the surface.

During bubblenet feeding, the whale locates an aggregation of prey, dives below, and discharges a line of bubbles from its blowholes while turning in a broad arc. As the bubbles ascend, they form a noisy visible ring or "net," which appears to disorient the prey. As the fish coalesce into a tight ball within the closing net, the whale

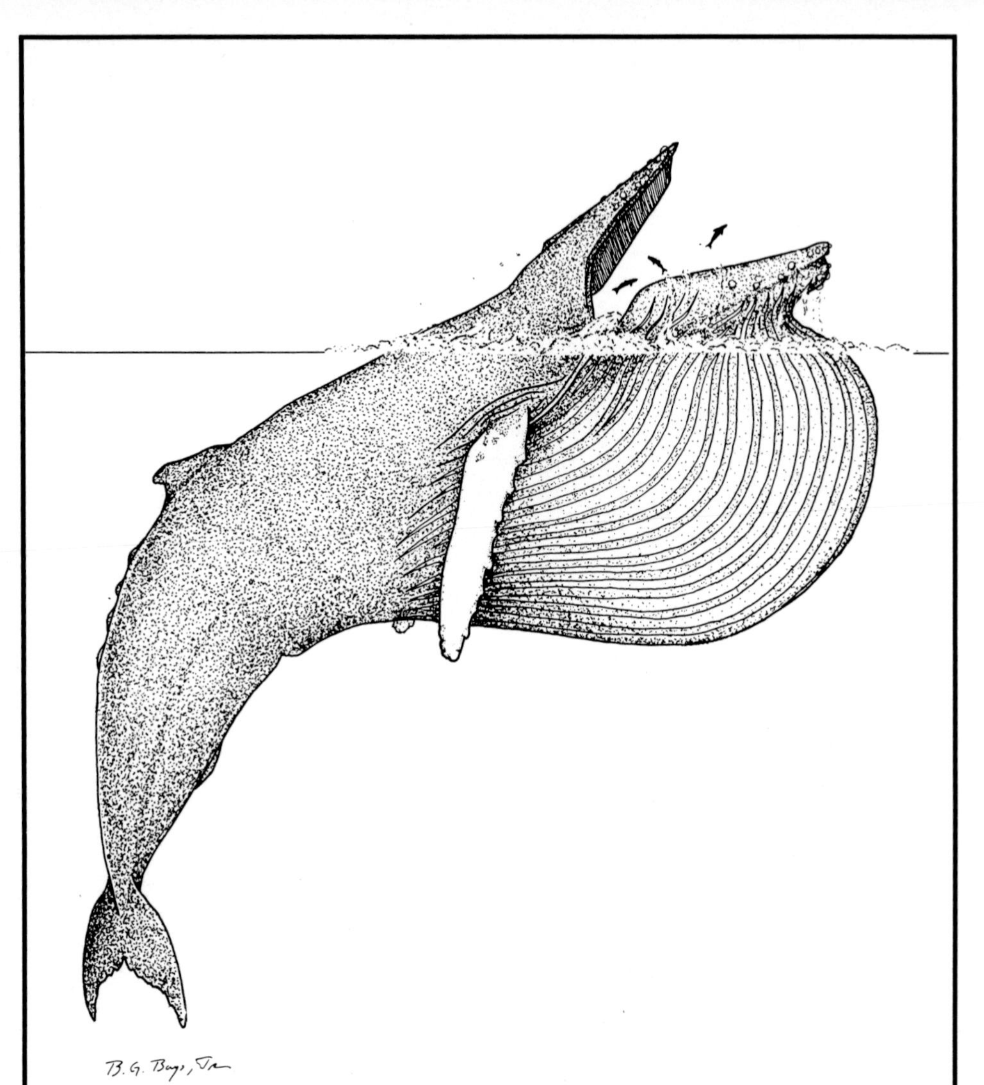

Distended ventral grooves of a feeding humpback.

rises from below, bursting through the surface with its mouth open, engulfing the concentrated food. The whale apparently swims towards the surface while releasing the bubbles, blocking the food on the sides, and pushing them up with its body. At the surface the bubbles appear as discrete basketball-size spheres. As the spheres join to form a ring, the food can be seen near its center. If the food is herring, it often times can be observed leaping into the air. Seabirds frequently dive-bomb the whales in order to capture the leaping fish. They are not always fast enough to avoid being swallowed themselves. Thoughts like these ran through our mind early one July afternoon in Alaska as we sat in a ten foot inflatable boat waiting for a group of feeding whales to surface. With a sound like percolating coffee, bubbles began to appear just off one side of our boat. We showed little concern until we began to realize that we were in the middle of the net and not beside it! As the net continued to close, a mad scramble ensued for the oars. We had just enough time to realize we

Humpbacks can consume nearly a ton of food in a day's time.

didn't have oars, when the bubble net ceased. The whales apparently decided they didn't like the taste of researchers, for they surfaced through another net thirty yards away.

A humpback can consume nearly a ton of food in a day's time. Whales feed opportunistically, engorging themselves when large concentrations of prey are found, and fasting between periods of plenty. These unpredictable periods of feeding and fasting fit in well with the annual cycle comprised of a general period of feeding, followed by a general period of fasting during the breeding season. Humpbacks are well-suited to this strategy of traveling long distances between areas of plentiful food and areas of more favorable temperature. Their blubber constitutes both a natural pantry and superb insulation against the cold.

CHAPTER THIRTEEN

Enemies and Parasites

The various knobs, folds, bumps and creases of a humpback's body play host to a variety of parasitic creatures. The most numerous and obvious **ectoparasites** are the **barnacles.** Barnacles come in a variety of sizes, shapes and colors, and can attach themselves directly to the skin, to other established barnacles, or can actually embed themselves in the flesh. The barnacles do not actually parasitize the whale, but use the whale as a base, allowing a better opportunity to feed on planktonic marine organisms.

The barnacles most often associated with humpbacks are the **acorn barnacles,** *Coronula diaderma* and *C. reginae.* They can be found attached to the flukes, flippers, head and the tubercles. Acorn barnacles flourish in the polar waters and then drop off in the warm waters of Hawaii, often leaving a white ring of scar tissue. Humpbacks have been found with as much as 1,000 pounds of acorn barnacles attached to them! Acorn barnacles seem to be attracted to humpbacks because of their relatively slow swimming speeds.

Another barnacle species, the **long-necked goose barnacle** *Conchorderma auritum,* is not as adept as the acorn barnacle in attaching to the whale's skin. It must rely on anchoring itself to established barnacles, and well-sheltered spots such as the ventral

OPPOSITE PAGE: Whale lice, *Cyamus boopis.*
TOP RIGHT: The highly social killer whale or orca, has been observed carrying out coordinated attacks on baleen whales including the humpback.
BOTTOM RIGHT: Acorn barnacles. *Cornula diaderma,* can attach themselves to various parts of the whale's body including the end of the pectoral fin.

grooves and genital slit. This barnacle also flourishes in the feeding grounds and drops off by the time its host has reached the warmer breeding grounds.

Near the base of the barnacles live small, pale, spidery parasitic animals which feed on the humpback's skin. These tiny crustaceans are the "whale lice" or **cyamids,** belonging to the family Cyamidae. The cyamids are not free-living. They survive only on whales, like many other species-specific whale lice. The humpback's unique species of whale lice *Cyamus boopis,* is about one inch long with strong claws attached to each of its ten legs. Other crustaceans, small **copepods** sometimes referred to as "water fleas," can be found living on the humpback's baleen plates among the end-bristles, and also burrowed deeply into the whale's flesh.

Microscopic organisms, such as **algae** and **diatoms,** flourish and bloom on the humpback's skin. Quite often, whales observed in Alaska, and new arrivals to Hawaii, have a yellowish-green tint to the lighter portions of their bodies. This tint effect is caused by green algae, and is quite striking on whales with all white tail flukes and pectoral fins.

Humpbacks host a variety of **endoparasites,** including round worms, tapeworms, flukes, and hookworms. Young humpbacks are susceptible to a urogenital-tract ailment caused by the worm-like

ABOVE: Although missing half its tail, this adult whale is able to signal aggression with powerful repeated tail slaps, and seems well able to defend itself against attack.

BELOW: Remoras frequently seen attached to the bodies of a variety of large whale species may help remove dead skin and ectoparasites. This would in part explain why numerous remoras are seen attached to the mother and not the newborn calf.

Whales of all ages are susceptible to parasitism. The subadult shown here (ABOVE & BELOW) has scars left by cookie cutter shark bites along the side of its body, and bloody flukes, perhaps resulting from harassment by pelagic sharks. The pigmentation of this whale is also highly unusual.

Crassicauda crassicauda. During the necropsy of a stranded two month old calf in Hawaii in 1981, twelve species of internal parasites were discovered.

A variety of **teleost** (bony) fish and shark species including the leather-back runner *(Scombroides sancti-petri)* and remora *(Remilegia australis)* are often observed swimming near or attached to humpbacks. They feed on bits of dead skin, algae, parasitic worms, and the small invertebrates attached to the whale's body. Many humpbacks have mysterious oval or round wounds and white scars on their heads, backs, and flanks. Since leatherback runners could not have caused such symmetrical scars it has been suggested that these markings are caused by remoras, squid, octopus, or sharks. It is likely that many of the scars result from a small nocturnal shark, *Isitius brasiliensis,* which is only two feet in length and has round fleshy suction-cup lips which allow it to attach to virtually any animal. Known as the **cookie-cutter shark,** it feeds by attaching to the humpback and sinking its teeth into the whale's flesh. As the whale swims, the water current and the whale's movements turn the shark slowly around enabling it to slice out a two inch deep circle of flesh, leaving behind a clean round scar.

Humpbacks are not threatened by terrestrial predators, other than man. In the sea the humpback faces only two natural threats, **sharks** and **killer whales.** Sharks are known to attack sick, distressed or injured animals. There has never been a reported attack of sharks on a healthy whale. While in Hawaii, humpback calves are the most likely to fall prey to sharks. The larger, **pelagic** (deep water) sharks of Hawaii, the tiger, hammerhead, and the Pacific gray, are the greatest threats.

The surface scars left by barnacles which normally fall off in warmer water can be contrasted with the more substantial wound left by the cookie cutter shark seen here in the photograph center as a deep solid white scar.

Scars left by attack from an orca are seen here as the evenly spaced dark lines across the white pigmentation of the flukes. Note also the unusual folding of the fluke tips.

In 1975, a newborn calf appeared in Molokini crater off the southern end of Maui without its mother. It was physically emaciated, as though it had not been fed for some time. The mother had either died or had abandoned her calf. After several days in Molokini, the calf became very weak. Soon an increasing number of sharks began to invade the crater. A large, ten foot tiger shark made an initial pass at the calf. When the weakened calf showed little ambition to defend itself, the shark tore off half of its left pectoral fin. In less than 20 minutes Molokini crater was a pool of blood and the near two-and-a-half ton calf was consumed.

Killer whales *(Orcinus orca)* are the only cetacean known to feed on other warm-blooded species. They survive on the flesh of fish, seals, penguins, dolphins and other whales. Sightings of killer whales, or orcas, in Hawaii have been reported but they are uncommon. The orca is quite gregarious and hunts in large pods. Recently we witnessed a pod of 5 orcas, one large male and 4 smaller ones, attack and consume several bottlenose dolphins off the east coast of Australia. Numerous accounts of orca attacking humpback whales have been found in the whaling literature. In 1982, Hal Whitehead of the Newfoundland Institute for Cold Ocean Science witnessed 12 orcas attacking two humpbacks off Newfoundland. In addition to this direct observation of orca predation, he estimated that 33% of all humpback flukes photographed off Newfoundland showed scars left by killer whale teeth. Scars resulting from apparent orca attacks have also been photographically recorded on a few humpbacks in Hawaii.

Hawaiian humpbacks are most likely preyed upon by killer whales while in the northwest Pacific. Hunting in coordinated groups, the killer whale renders its victim defenseless by removing portions of the flippers and flukes. Feeding usually involves tearing long strips of flesh from the helpless whale. Killer whales seem to prefer the tongues of great whales, and have been observed to force open the mouth of a dead whale and tear out its tongue.

Humpbacks are not defenseless against such attacks. They will use their massive tail flukes as a weapon, thrashing out at the attacker. Such observations have been made by Graham Chittleborough in Australia. They can also use their elongated rostrum to ram headlong into an opponent. Humpbacks can also affiliate with other nearby whales or attempt to outswim and out-dive their predators. Adult humpbacks have some refuge in size but calves are probably most vulnerable when they reach the Alaskan waters.

ABOVE: Killer whales, the only cetacean known to feed regularly on other marine mammals, pose a formidable threat to large whales. Sightings of orca on the Hawaiian breeding grounds are extremely rare.
LEFT: Extensive damage to the flukes (center left) may slow the whale down and lead to increased parasitism by other organisms such as body lice, which can be seen as a large orange patch on the tail stock (lower left). LOWER RIGHT: The setting sun in southeastern Alaska highlights the algal growth on the white flukes of this diving whale.

CHAPTER FOURTEEN

Age

How long do humpback whales live? Unfortunately it is not possible to provide a direct answer to this question. Past research on **age determination** has been carried out on animals killed during whaling operations and for scientific study. Of course this only tells us how old the animal was when it was killed and not how long it would have lived otherwise. Scientists have tried many ways to determine the age of individual whales. Age determination is important in answering questions about birth rates, distribution of age classes, and death rates, which ultimately tell us whether the population is increasing or decreasing.

One method of age determination discovered by Norwegian and Russian biologists in the 1940s is based upon annual changes in the growth rate of baleen plates. It has been determined that as the baleen plates grow through periods of feeding and fasting during each year, slight but detectable variations in their thickness occur. By counting the series of grooves and ridges across the plates, estimates were made of the age of the whales brought aboard whaling ships. Unfortunately, this method is valid only up to about six years of age, because wear at the tip of the continually growing plates makes determination unreliable beyond this stage.

A second method for determining age is to examine the reproductive organs. The ovaries of females bear a scar *(corpus albicans)* on the surface following the release of each egg (see page 32). Biologists have shown that the rate of accumulation of these scars can be correlated with increases in body size and presumably increased age. But there is considerable variation in the age at which females first ovulate, and these scars become more difficult to differentiate in older females.

Biologists are not even certain how many ovulations occur each year. For all these reasons, counting scars allows only the determination of whether one whale is older than another but does little to tell us about the specific age of either. The age of male humpbacks has been estimated by weighing the testes in conjunction with measuring the degree of ossification of the vertebral column (as mammals age, certain vertebrae begin to fuse). This method tends to be inaccurate because a male's testes can vary widely within a year depending upon reproductive state once sexual maturity has been attained.

A third way to determine the age of a humpback is to examine its ear canals. Most mammals excrete a waxy substance from the inner ear which is eventually displaced through the external ear opening. The humpback's tiny external ear opening which prevents water from pouring in, also stops the waxy excretion from moving out. As a result, the ear wax builds upon itself forming a solid plug filling the auditory canal. This **ear plug** attains the length of nearly three feet in adults. If the ear plug is sliced in half along its longitudinal axis, each year's layer of wax can be differentiated from the next. In fact, one is able to see alternating light and dark layers which are laid down during periods of rapid growth associated with summer

A front view of a feeding humpback showing the baleen plates suspended from the upper jaw. In the past, baleen was used to determine the age of humpbacks.

feeding, and periods of slower growth caused by winter fasting. By counting the layers or laminations, an estimate of the whales age may be derived. Unfortunately, not all layers are clearly distinguished—especially those laid down early in life. The laminations produced in years of high food consumption are much more noticeable than those produced in leaner years. Even periods of pregnancy and lactation can influence the ability to distinguish the laminations. Consequently this is a very inexact method for determining age.

In spite of the vagaries in estimating age using the techniques just described, biologists have estimated the following general parameters for life cycle development in humpbacks. Puberty is reached at about 2 - 4 years of age, with sexual or reproductive maturity following in the next 1 - 2 years. Both sexes continue to grow through the early stages of adulthood, reaching physical maturity between 10 - 12 years of age.

It must be emphasized that these estimates are derived from a number of different studies in which biologists have shown little agreement in applying admittedly unreliable techniques. Bear in mind that at the time these methods were developed, the intent was to find better ways to efficiently harvest the mature whales while leaving the breeding stock intact. Much of the so-called age determination work, therefore, was more directly an attempt to relate maturity of development to average body size. In fact, average body size within and between sexes can vary quite considerably at a given age.

Humpbacks appear to live for 30 or 40 years, although the maximum range can be considerably higher. One female in the South Pacific was estimated to be at least 50 years of age at the time she was killed. This brings us back to the original point that methods of age determination used in the past seem of little value today because they are dependent upon killing the whale. The current use of photographic identification allows the development of life histories of known individuals. This will eventually lead to more precise answers to questions about age while leaving the population unharmed.

CHAPTER FIFTEEN
Identification

The identification of individual whales is one important way to determine movement patterns, life histories, and social interactions of individual whales as well as the groups in which they are found. Prior to the 1970s research scientists tracked humpback whales using numbered stainless-steel darts known as **Discovery Tags.** These darts were fired into the dorsal musculature to be recovered during processing after the whale was killed. Whaling biologists operating in the southern hemisphere during the first half of the century shot nearly 5,000 Discovery Tags into humpbacks. Fewer than three percent were ever recovered. Even these provided no information about movements of animals during the period between marking by scientists and capture by the whaling ships. Most often the animals were killed not far from the original marking spot, often within days or weeks of being tagged. Determination of specific migratory routes was next to impossible as there was no way to establish whether the animal had ever left the area even after months or years passed between marking and capture.

Many attempts have been made to develop long-term visible tags for large

whales. These include: branding (impractical for large species which cannot be handled easily), streamer tags (often dislodged by water turbulence), and dye (it usually washes away). In the last few years radio-tagging has been employed with success on a number of large and small cetaceans. These tags are either mounted on the dorsal fin, anchored subcutaneously, or attached by a suction cup. There have been, however, a number of intrinsic drawbacks associated with each type of tag used. A useful tag must meet a number of criteria.

1) the tag is ineffective if it damages the animal or enhances mortality.

2) the tag should not cause the animal to become isolated from or avoided by its conspecifics.

3) the tag should remain in place for an extended period of time.

4) the tag should be easily recovered or highly visible.

Because of a failure to meet some or all of these criteria, limited results have been derived from the various tags described. Technical problems such as short battery life, equipment failure, and difficulty in receiving and transmitting broadcast signals have also limited the use of radio tags to date. However, anticipated technological advances in the reduction of size and weight of the transmitters, coupled with increased access to satellites, should improve radio-tracking techniques and the quality of data gathered.

In 1979 Steve Katona and his colleagues, working off the New England coast, established that the conspicuous coloration patterns of humpbacks are of special importance in long-term tracking studies of free-living whales. They noted that each humpback has unique markings and coloration patterns on the ventral surface of its tail. As with the human fingerprint, no two whales possess the same **fluke print.** Ventral fluke coloration varies from all white to all black, with an infinite variety of mottled black-and-white patterns in between (see photos left). Many animals also have permanent scars on their flukes caused by sharks, killer whales, the scraping of rock, or barnacles on the bodies of other whales (pages 60-61). Whales have even been seen with large portions of the tail missing (pages 58 and 62).

Different humpback fluke patterns ranging from light to dark.

When a humpback dives after a series of respirations at the surface, it frequently lifts its tail out of the water in a fluke-up dive (page 83), revealing the pattern on the ventral surface of the tail. Researchers photograph the ventral portion of the tail, and compile a catalog of fluke identifications complete with information about the sighting (date, time, pod composition, travel direction, presence/absence of a calf, etc.)

Using this procedure more than a thousand humpback whales have been individually identified in Hawaiian waters. Although only a relatively small number of whales have been re-identified on subsequent occasions, these fluke photographs will be instrumental in yielding new insights into migratory routes, population estimates, social structure and behavior, longevity, sexual maturity, and reproductive rate. *But much more importantly, fluke identification photographs have removed the need to kill whales in order to study and understand them.*

The use of fluke patterns for individual identification works only with subadults and adults. The tail patterns of calves are milky-white and do not "set" in an established pattern until after the first year or two of life. A method for identifying calves using underwater photographs of the lip grooves has been established by Deborah Glockner. Each side of the whale's head can have anywhere from one to six lip grooves extending from the corner of the mouth to the pectoral fin (see diagram pg. 21). The number of grooves on each side of the head, which may or may not be the same, in conjunction with the sex of the animal permits unique identification of individual calves. This procedure is a useful but challenging one since it requires underwater photographs of each identified calf's head.

Humpbacks may also be identified on the basis of dorsal fin shape and body scarring. Dorsal fins of humpback whales come in an endless variety of shapes, ranging from high, curved fins to inconspicuous bumps. Photographs of the right and left views of the dorsal fin can help to identify whales when no fluke photograph is available. Such identification is made difficult by the changing appearance of the dorsal fin as the whale rounds-out and dives. Quite often, the job can be made easier when the dorsal fin is heavily scarred on one side and/or the other, or in rare cases where part of the fin has been removed, leaving a notch-shaped

ABOVE: The same whale originally tagged photographically in S.E. Alaska in 1982 is photographed again in Hawaii in 1985.
BELOW: Whales may also be identified by unique dorsal fin shapes and markings.

Researchers from the Pacific Whale Foundation have recently shown that South Pacific humpbacks may be identified by pigmentation patterns extending high up on the sides of the body.

cleft. Body scars obtained from contact with rocks, anchor lines, ships' bows, sharks, killer whales, humpbacks, and other cetaceans are like tattoos which can be used to identify individual whales.

Humpback whales also display variations in black and white patterns on the ventral and lateral surfaces of their body. Four lateral body pigmentation types have been defined for humpbacks ranging from nearly all white to all black. While we have observed all four body types in our research in the southern hemisphere, whales in Hawaii have little or no white markings on their sides. The coloration pattern of the pectoral fins are generally not used in the identification process although they are subject to a great deal of scarring. In general, the pectoral fins are not as easy to observe as the dorsal fin and tail. Nonetheless, special notations are made in the fluke catalog when a whale has distinct pectoral fins, such as a unique scar, white coloration or conspicuous damage.

Although pigmentation, scar, and lip groove patterns are useful in discovering the life history of individual animals by tracking their movements and social interactions for protracted periods, they do not indicate the whale's sex. Howard Winn, a zoologist at the University of Rhode Island, has developed a technique for sexing live cetaceans using analysis of chromosomal material found in all the body's cells. Females of most mammalian species are characterized by having two 'x' chromosomes, but they only need one. The second one, which becomes inactive is called a **barr body.** Its presence in tissue collected for analysis identifies the whale from which it came as a female, at least in humpbacks. Certain species, such as the minke whale, do not appear to show this characteristic. Material for analysis is collected by firing a hollow six inch biopsy dart into a surfacing whale's side. A piece of line attached to the dart allows it to be retrieved. The tip of the dart is configured in such a way that when it is

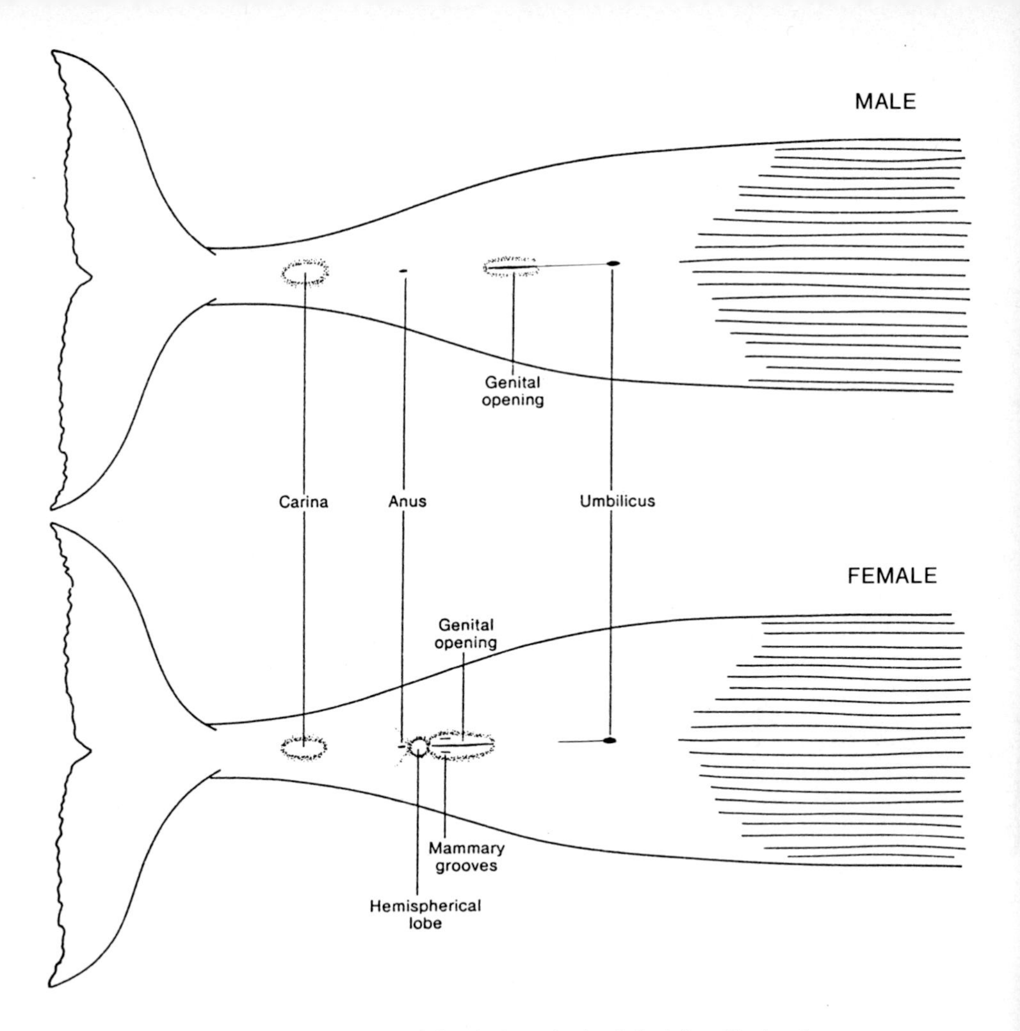

Diagram of the genital area of a male and female humpback whale (after Glockner),

pulled out of the whale a small core sample of tissue is obtained which can later be stained and cytologically tested. The method seems simple, but a number of difficulties render it costly and inefficient. Research is continuing in order to enhance the method's success.

There are few easily noticed differences between male and female humpbacks. It has been suggested that males are more likely to have a white stripe due to scarring along the dorsal fin and caudal peduncle. Since not all males are likely to have this characteristic and it has yet to be shown that females never have it, the hypothesis remains questionable. However, differences between the sexes are found on the ventral surface. The distance between the genital opening and the anus is almost 2.5 times greater in males than in females. The genital opening of males is more anterior than that of females, while the female's genital opening is surrounded by a thick wall adorned with a golf-ball-sized swelling called the hemispherical lobe. Underwater photographs of the lateral and/or ventral views of a humpback clearly show the hemispherical lobe in the female and its absence in males (see photo pg. 120). This technique is an important discovery, but it is far from an easy procedure. Taking a picture of the genital opening of a humpback whale is like lying on a highway and trying to get a photograph of the oil pan of a semi-trailer truck as it passes.

CHAPTER SIXTEEN

Communication and Song

Cetaceans, like all animals, have had to develop a method of communication suited to their environment. At depths vision becomes limited, and yelling over the tops of waves while at the surface can be extremely energy consuming. Sound travels three times faster underwater than in air, with low frequencies traveling the furthest. The increased speed of sound in water makes it an ideal medium for communication. While all cetaceans are able to emit sounds under a variety of conditions, the humpback whale seems unique in the complex diversity of its underwater vocalizations.

Humpbacks produce a wide array of sounds, including the highest and the lowest frequencies humans can hear, with an extraordinary range of tonal qualities. How humpbacks create these sounds is unknown since they do not have functional vocal cords. Some evidence suggests that the sounds are produced by various valves, muscles, and a series of blind sacs found branching off the respiratory tract. Most of

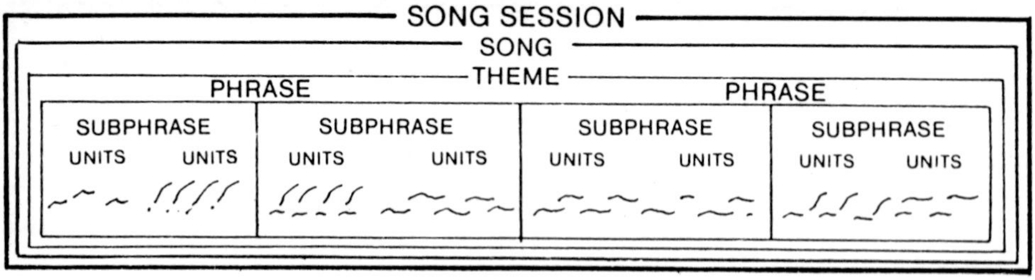

SONG SESSION
SONG
THEME
PHRASE PHRASE
SUBPHRASE SUBPHRASE SUBPHRASE SUBPHRASE
UNITS UNITS UNITS UNITS UNITS UNITS UNITS UNITS

The humpback whale's song is a highly structured series of vocalizations as demonstrated here.

the sounds produced by humpbacks form long, complex patterns which are often repeated for hours.

Humpback whale sounds were first reported in 1952 by O.W. Schreiber on the basis of recordings collected at the U.S. Navy Sound Fixing and Ranging Station (SOFAR), Kaneohe Bay, Hawaii. In 1958 Alex Kibblewhite, working for the New Zealand Navy, described similar sounds as the "barnyard chorus," and noted their coincidence with the annual migration of humpback whales through New Zealand waters. In 1967, Frank Watlington, a U.S. Naval acoustic engineer, made recordings of humpback whale sounds he had collected in Bermuda available to biologist Roger Payne, who later reported with Scott McVay that the sounds of humpback whales were organized into repeating patterns which they described as "songs." Soon after, Katy Payne found that the humpback song displayed a characteristic without precedent among non-humans. It showed a constant and progressive change from year to year, unlike the songs of birds.

A humpback song is composed of a series of discrete notes or **units.** A unit is the shortest discrete sound noticeable to the human ear. A series of units constitutes a **phrase.** Phrases are usually uniform in duration, and may contain repeated sounds. A consecutive group of phrases make up a **theme.** Although a given theme may vary in the number of phrases it contains, the sequence of its phrases is always the same. Similarly the sequence in which themes occur is always the same, although some themes may be left out. A predictable series of themes forms a **song.** A song generally lasts between 6 and 18 minutes, depending on the number of phrases it includes. A sequence of songs in which there are no pauses greater than one minute, is a **song session.** A whale may cycle through many songs without a pause; we once recorded a whale in Hawaii that sang for 14 hours without stopping. It was still singing when we left it.

The whale's song is in a constant state of evolution. As the season progresses, new themes may be introduced or old ones may be changed. Each singer changes its song to keep in tune with other singers. As a result the song heard at the end of the season is quite different from the song heard at the beginning. Little or no singing takes place during the summer and further change to the song does not appear to occur. When the whales return to Hawaii the following winter, they resume singing the version in vogue at the end of the previous breeding season. The song continues to change as years go by. After five years the song is hardly recognizable compared with its earlier form. To date, song components that have been dropped have never reappeared.

The Paynes believe that all the whales in the eastern North Pacific sing the same song. They have found that whales in Hawaii sing the same song as whales found around the Revillagigedo Islands of Mexico, some 3,000 miles away. Photographic identification of flukes has established that a small number of whales have "switched" breeding grounds, traveling both to Hawaii and Mexico in different years. It is understandable then that songs in both areas would be similar. What is not as easily explained is how identical changes to the song occur within a season across such a great expanse of ocean. Perhaps the song is learned on the feeding grounds where animals from the different breeding grounds mix and the occasional song is heard.

Because singing occurs primarily during the breeding season, Kenneth Norris proposed in 1966 that the song serves a reproductive function. The exact way in which it accomplishes this is unknown, but it has been shown that only the males sing (see Social Dynamics pg 112). This is not to say that all males sing; it has not yet been possible to determine which segment of the male population engages in the behavior. The song may serve to attract females, scare away other males, or maintain the distance between singers. The length and number of singing bouts increase as the season progresses, with the maximum number of singers being heard during the latter half of the breeding season.

Observing a singing whale is a rare and impressive experience. We have watched whales singing in Hawaii, Fiji, American Samoa, Tonga and Australia. In each case the behavior was similar. The singing whale was found suspended head down some 50 -75 feet below the surface. With its eyes closed and its tail pointed skyward, it remained motionless save for the slow movement of its pectoral fins forward and back, looking much like an opera singer swinging his arms to help hit those high and low notes. A singing whale typically stays down for 15 minutes or so, then surfaces within 200 yards of its last surface location. As it rises to the surface, a noticeable attenuation in the song occurs. This makes it possible on some occasions to determine which whale is doing the singing. However, while snorkeling underwater, localization of a singing whale is extremely difficult. Even when next to a singing whale the sound appears to be coming from all directions. The song vibrates through the body because of its powerful amplification. The experience of being next to a singing whale is like standing beside the pipes of an organ in a massive cathedral.

On a number of occasions in Hawaii we have observed a singing male humpback escorting a mother and calf. On one of these occasions the escort continued to sing as the trio moved along the coastline, so loudly that we could actually hear the song above the noise of our outboard motor as we traveled slowly along behind them. On another of these occasions, we were in the water with a mother and calf when the escort whale swam right beneath us and began to sing!

There is little doubt that the song is an important form of communication. Exactly what is communicated remains in question. Humpbacks do make other sounds which are associated with feeding and socially active groups. Such sounds are made by males and females alike and do not appear to be characterized by the elaborate patterns and complex organization found in the song. In short, the **social sounds** seem to function in much the same way as the vocalizations of other mammals, serving to communicate messages of biological urgency. On one occasion in 1980, we recorded sounds created by a mother and calf hovering just below the surface. While we were unable to determine whether the mother or the calf was making the sounds, we believe that continued opportunistic observation of such incidents could tell us much about the importance of learning and imitiation in the development of vocalization capabilities.

Research on the humpback whale song continues, with recent findings suggesting that each singer has its own voice pattern or signature. The song itself is perplexing with each discovery posing many new questions. The song is comprised of patterned transitions built on a bedrock of permanent structure. Some changes occur over many years while others alter the song within a brief period of time. The larger the sample of songs that are studied, the more complex the subtleties and sources of variety become. The question remains whether it is even possible to understand the full nature of the song, or any other vocalization patterns, without observing behavioral changes that occur in direct correlation with variation of the sounds. One of the more serious drawbacks of song research has been an inability to observe identified singers over repeated song sessions, or to study how individual songs change in relation to the "typical" song of a particular season.

CHAPTER SEVENTEEN

Status

It would be misleading to discuss the status of humpback whales without first pointing out that most population figures for marine mammals are a "best guess." Cetaceans are extremely difficult to count because they spend a fair amount of time underwater—humpbacks spend about *70% of their life* below the surface! In addition, the great whales, like the humpback, often travel alone or in small **pods** (groups) making them difficult to sight. It remains indisputable nevertheless, that the humpback whale is a rare and endangered species. More sophisticated mathematical models, and the use of photographic and radio telemetry tags, are currently under development and will ultimately provide much more accurate population estimates.

We will probably never know how many humpbacks there were before whaling. Humpbacks were hunted in the Northern Hemisphere until 1966, at which time they were afforded international protection from commercial whaling. Humpback

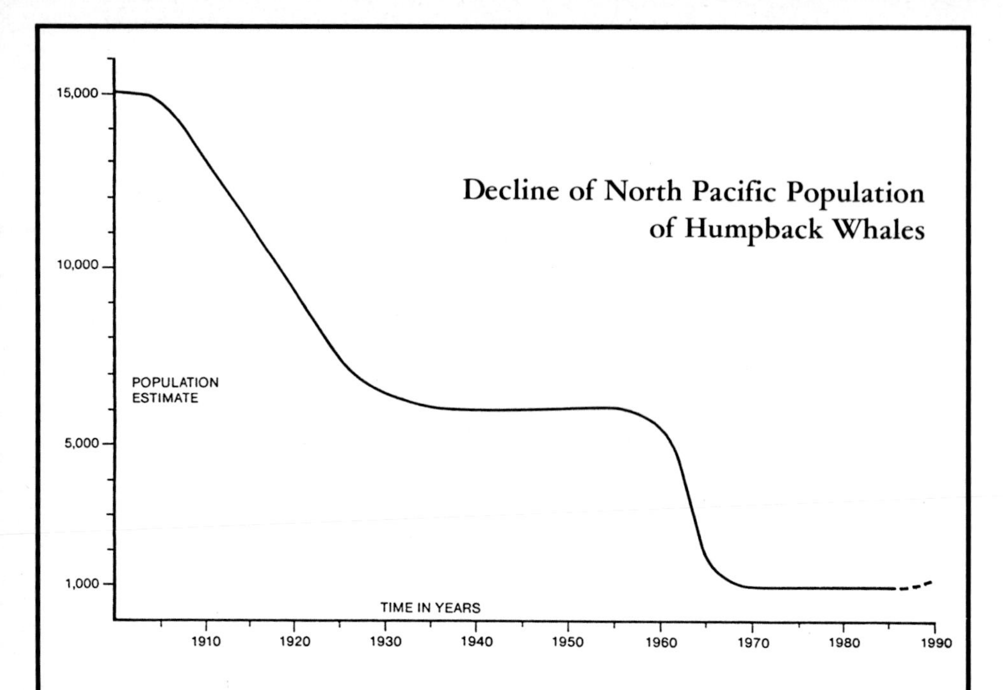

whales are only hunted today for subsistence purposes in a few remote areas. This probably results in fewer than 25 humpback whale deaths per year. None of these are known to occur in the North Pacific. The likelihood of whaling commencing on humpbacks again is poor, since a ban on all commercial whaling began in 1986.

Because of their slow swimming speeds and tendency to concentrate near accessible coastal areas in both the winter breeding and summer feeding grounds, humpbacks easily fell prey to early whalers. The worldwide estimate of humpbacks prior to the onslaught of intensive whaling has been given as 200,000. The present total lies somewhere between 5,000 - 10,000 animals; less than 5 percent of the original population.

The population estimate for the North Pacific stock has been placed at 15,000 animals for 1905. By mid-1910 commercial harvesting of humpbacks began in earnest on an international scale. By 1930, the North Pacific stock had dwindled to 6,000 animals. Between 1930 and 1960 humpbacks were taken at the rate of only 250 per year. However, in only five years, between 1960 and 1965, whaling fleets killed 5,000 humpbacks in the North Pacific. In 1966, a ban on hunting humpbacks in the Northern Hemisphere was proclaimed by the International Whaling Commission (the Southern Hemisphere stock had come under protection in 1963). At that time, it was estimated that fewer than 1,000 humpback whales remained. By 1986, the North Pacific stock was said to be somewhere in the order of 1,500 whales, with specific estimates ranging between 800 and 2,000 animals. Approximately 60% (480 - 1200) of these were in Hawaii that winter.

CHAPTER EIGHTEEN

Behavior Key

The following key lists a variety of behaviors frequently seen among humpback whales in Hawaii. Each behavior is categorized according to whether it is a group or individual behavior: in the case of individual behaviors, it is further categorized according to the body part involved. Brief definitions of the behavioral terms are provided, and where possible, the behavior is illustrated by photograph. Several of the terms are self-explanatory; others are more obscure. While some were coined by whalers of days gone by, others have been recently developed by scientists in order to specify more exactly the wide range of behaviors of interest. Because not all researchers use precisely the same terminology (or indeed, even recognize the same gradations of behavior), we present the key in the hopes of providing a degree of consistency and completeness for the reader's benefit. Our key is an expanded version of a behavioral list developed by the University of Hawaii's Kewalo Basin Marine Mammal Laboratory in 1976. While some of the terms will undoubtedly not achieve universal agreement, the list is comprehensive enough to adequately describe the behaviors most likely to be observed in Hawaii.

Group Behaviors

A. SLOW - MEDIUM - FAST SWIM: A group of whales appears at the surface at regular intervals. After 2 - 3 minutes of surface activity, the whales submerge for an extended period, then resurface some distance from the last point at which they were seen. Normally, surfacing intervals and locations are highly predictable. Swimming speed and direction can be affected by the presence of boats, aircraft, and other whales. Surfacing bouts appear to involve all the whales in a group, although not all whales will necessarily surface at exactly the same time; part of the group may surface and blow, with the remainder surfacing immediately after the first animals submerge. This can often make it difficult to determine the exact number of whales in a group, if there are more than four or five, and observations are being made from a boat.

A slow swim for a humpback is anything less than 2 - 3 mph; a medium swim from 3 - 8 mph, and a fast swim anything over 8 mph. Speeds over 8 mph occur for relatively short periods of time. Swimming speeds during migration average between 3 and 8 mph.

B. SURFACE TRAVELING: A group of whales remains at the surface while swimming for an extended period of time. This is most often seen with larger groups of more than three whales. Frequently, surface traveling pods engage in a variety of individual behaviors, remaining underway while doing so.

C. MILLING: A group of whales remains at the surface for an extended period of time, with no apparent progress in a specific directional heading being made. A wide range of activities, from rather sedate to highly charged, may occur in milling groups.

D. RESTING: A term usually applied to a single whale, or a mother and calf, observed remaining quietly in the same location for an extended period of time. Often the whale's back can be seen throughout the resting episode, although on many occasions, the whale may slowly submerge after rising to the surface to breathe, and remain hidden below the water before surfacing again in the same location some time later. Humpback whales do not rest in this fashion in groups, although it is possible that slow swimming groups may be engaging in a form of resting behavior.

E. AFFILIATION/DISAFFILIATION: Humpbacks in Hawaii, with the exception of a mother and her calf, generally form very transient, apparently short-lived groups. Whales are said to affiliate when they come together to interact, however briefly, and to disaffiliate when the interaction is terminated and one or more of the whales leave(s) the pod.

F. COALESCENCE/DISPERSAL: Pods of whales may change their within pod distance from each other as a function of the particular activity in which they are engaged, or as a result of approach by other whales or other species (including humans).

Individual Behaviors

RESPIRATION

A. **BLOW**: Normal pattern of exhalation and inhalation at the surface. Breathing occurs through the paired blowhole openings on the top of the head. The term refers to both the act of breathing and the cloud of water droplets produced above the animals head during the process of exhalation. (See Breathing, p. 33).

B. **NO-BLOW RISE**: Often the humpback will surface without making an audible blow, or producing the characteristic plume-like cloud. Such a "silent surfacing" is referred to as a no-blow rise.

C. **UNDERWATER BLOW**: Humpbacks do not always wait until their blowholes clear the surface before they exhale, Whales that are moving at relatively fast speeds, or surfacing and diving quickly, will frequently begin to exhale just before their head breaks the surface, creating a small explosion of frothing water.

D. **BUBBLING**: Humpbacks often release continuous, controlled amounts of air from both the mouth and blowholes. (It is generally assumed that air released from the mouth has been "gulped" at the surface, since humpbacks do not breathe

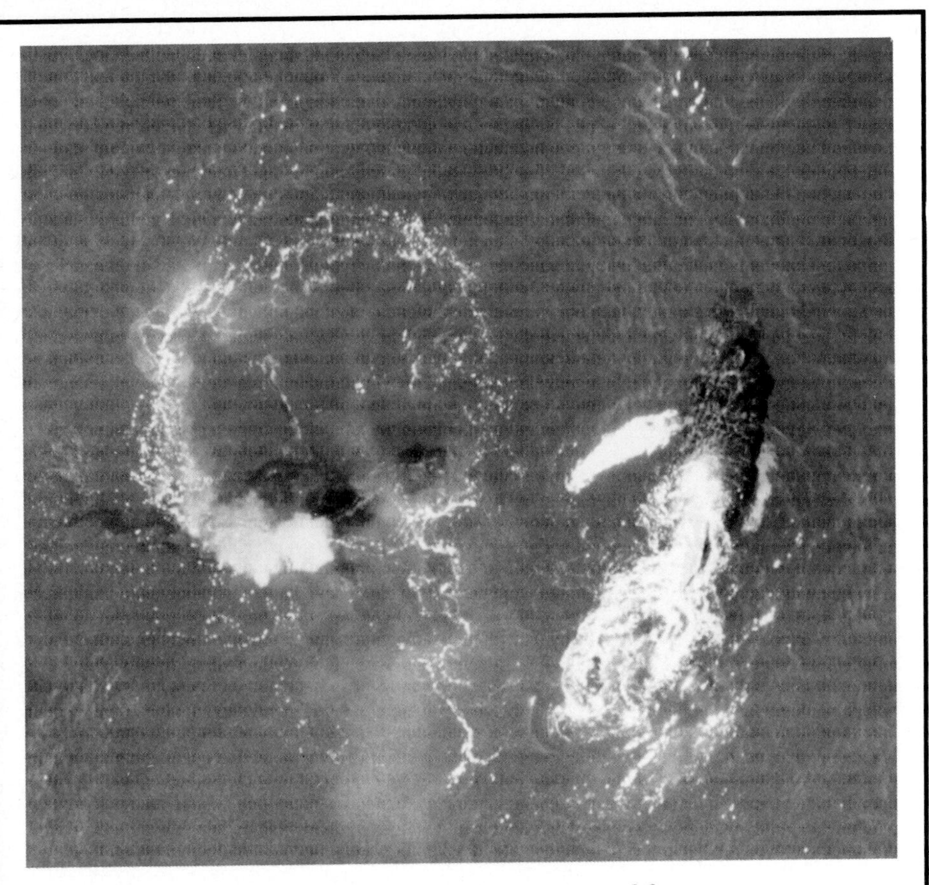

through their mouths.) Such bubbling takes a variety of forms.

Bubble trail. A bubble trail is created by the release of air from the blowholes or mouth while the whale is still underwater. The trail begins at the blowhole openings or corners of the mouth as two distinct lines, which quickly fuse into a chain of small bubbles stretching out 50 yards or more behind the whale (*see also* photo pg. 126).

Bubble screen. A controlled, intermittent release of air from the blowholes while the whale is underwater, which results in a thick cloud of small bubbles less than 0.25 inches in diameter. This differs from a bubble trail in that the bubbles are localized in a contained, relatively small area.

Bubble net. A controlled, underwater release of air from the blowholes carried out while the whale swims or turns in a circle of approximately 30 - 40 feet in diameter. The bubbles of air rise to the surface and burst, forming a spiralling trail. This is a behavior associated with feeding activity and is observed in its most distinct form only on the feeding grounds (see Feeding, p. 50).

POSTURES

A. ROUND OUT/PEDUNCLE ARCH/SLIP UNDER: Whales often breathe more than once after surfacing, often as many as three to five times within a brief two or three minute period. Following the last inhalation, the whale begins a diving descent by arching its body slightly, while rolling ahead at the surface. This is referred to as the **round out.** As the caudal peduncle appears at the surface, the whale may arch it high above the water, perhaps in an attempt to dive more deeply. This is called the

peduncle arch (above right). If the whale submerges without rounding out and/or arching the peduncle, it is called a **slip under** (above left).

B. FLUKE UP DIVE/FLUKE DOWN DIVE: Following a peduncle arch, the humpback will usually bring its tail flukes above the surface of the water as it dives almost

straight down. In a **fluke up dive** (above left), the tail flukes will be brought straight up into the air, exposing the entire ventral surface, showing the unique pattern of markings found on each whale. In a **fluke down dive** (above right), the flukes are brought clear of the water, but remain turned down, so the ventral surface is not exposed. In Hawaii, adults frequently do fluke up dives; calves virtually never do.

C. SNAKING: We infrequently see whales engaging in an S-shaped postural display we have termed **snaking.** In this posture, the anterior portion of the head is angled

up out of the water, the dorsal fin is just above the surface, the peduncle is arched just below the water, and the flukes are kept underwater. It seems a very peculiar, almost impossible, posture for a large whale to assume. This unusual behavior is done while the whale is swimming at the surface, and is held only briefly. Occurrences have not been observed frequently enough to allow us to hypothesize as to the significance of the display.

D. MOTORBOATING: The whale swims rapidly at the surface with its head angled above the water with the rest of the body parallel to the surface. As the whale moves along in this position, the head creates a visible wake much like that created by the hull of a boat moving through the water.

HEAD DISPLAYS

A. SPY HOP: The whale rises relatively straight up out of the water rather slowly, maintains its head above the surface to just below the eye, often turns 90 - 180 degrees on its longitudinal axis, then slips back below the surface (right).

B. HEAD RISE: The head is brought up above the surface of the water at an approximately 45 - 90 degree angle. Generally, the eye is not exposed. Mouth may sometimes be partially inflated.

C. HEAD LUNGE: The head is brought above the surface of the water at an approximate 0 - 45 degree angle while the whale lunges forward with a momentary burst of speed. Often the humpback will expand or inflate its mouth by filling it with water, perhaps in an attempt to increase its apparent size. The display is generally carried out broadside to another whale. We have also observed whales inflating their mouths underwater, dramatically increasing their girth.

D. HEAD SLAP: The head slap is an exciting display of the humpback's power and size. Propelling half of its body out of the water in a nearly perpendicular direction, the whale pounds its massive, sometimes partially engorged mouth back down onto the water's surface, sending out explosions of water around its head. The head will rise nearly 20 ft above the water at the peak of the display. Some have referred to the head slap as a breach, or incomplete form of breach, but we reserve that term for another behavior which we believe to be functionally distinct from the head slap.

E. BUTTING: Male humpback whales use their ponderous, oversized heads to push each other out of the way as they jostle for position in the pod. This is carried out by rising up out of the water beside another whale, and then forcing the ventral surface of the head down on the dorsal surface of the competitor's head. It has been suggested that the jaw plate on the end of the lower jaw, which is often encrusted with barnacles, may be used to enhance the effect of the maneuver. Whales on the receiving end of such attacks end up with their head scarred and bleeding, especially on the surface of the sensory nodules.

F. HEAD SHAKE: Both above and below the water's surface, humpbacks display a behavior that has been seen in many species of dolphins, and is associated with threatening. The whale (as the dolphin) shakes its head quickly from side to side while swimming toward another whale. Cetaceans, with few exceptions, have fused neck vertebrae, making the side to side movement look much like a quick and violent twitch or jerk.

F. JAW CLAP: Humpbacks signal stress, and perhaps anger, by a violent clapping of the lower jaw against the upper. While this is not often seen above the surface, it has been noted in both adults and calves underwater.

H. EYE WIDENING: The humpback's eye is not usually fully visible. Generally, it does not clear the surface of the water long enough to be observed in air, and from a distance it is obscured by thick folds of skin which almost completely cover it. Underwater, the eye appears only as a darkened opening in these folds. On occasion, however, the eye appears to bulge and widen, exposing the white around the iris. In dolphins, such eye widening is a sure sign of stress

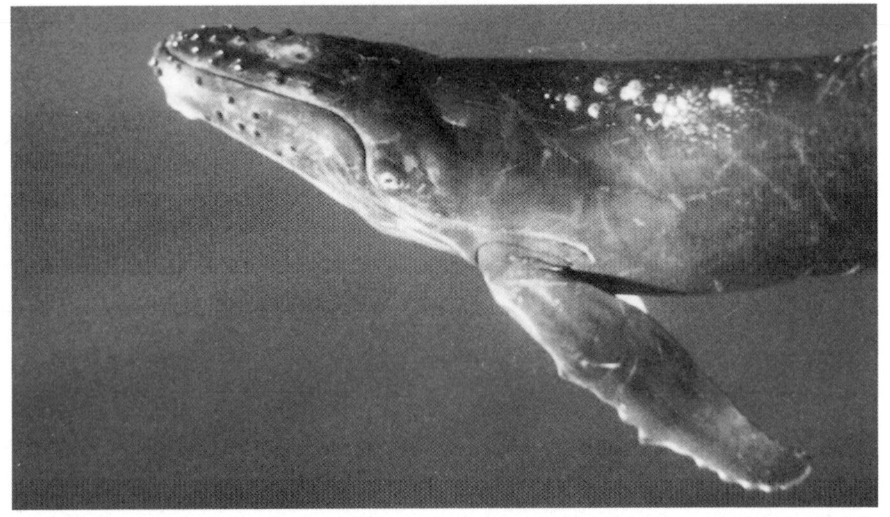

induced by either fear or anger, and it is likely that the same is true of the humpback. This behavior occurs underwater, and would be seen by most people only in underwater photographs and film footage.

PECTORAL FIN DISPLAYS

A. PEC EXTENSION/PEC WAVE: The pectoral fins are often extended high up into the air while the whale is lying at the surface, either on its back or side. Sometimes the whale will simply hold one pec, or flipper, straight up while lying on its side, with the end of one side of the fluke also exposed. (Whale-watchers may mistake the exposed portion of the fluke for the pec fin of a calf). At other times, the whale will lie on its back and wave both pec fins back and forth in the air.

B. **PEC RUBBING:** Refers to the rubbing or stroking along the body of another whale with the pectoral fins. In courting pods observed from the air, one humpback may be observed swimming through the extended pec fins of a second whale lying on its side. Such encounters involve extensive contact with the pectoral fins. We have even observed a subadult humpback directing such behaviors at a singularly unimpressed northern right whale.

C. **PEC SLAP (FLIPPER FLOP):** Humpbacks frequently roll at the surface, slapping their long pectoral fins against the water, or they may lie on their side, bringing one fin high up into the air and then swinging it forcefully down onto the surface of the water with a resounding smack. We have also observed whales lying on their back waving both fins in the air at the same time, before slapping them on top of the water. In general, it does not appear that pec slapping is an aggressive activity, and may actually be an invitational display.

TAIL (FLUKE) DISPLAYS

A. **TAIL WAVE/FLUKE EXTENSION:** A display in which the flukes and caudal peduncle are extended straight up into the air, with the animal's head pointed directly toward the ocean floor. The flukes may be gently waved back and forth **(tail wave)**, or simply held motionless in the air **(fluke extension)**.

B. TAIL COCK: While the whale is lying upright in the water (i.e., with its dorsal surface exposed), the caudal peduncle is bent and slightly arched at its posterior extremity, so that the flukes are curled down, giving the impression of a slingshot about to be released. This behavior occurs while the whale is stationary at the surface.

C. TAIL SLASH: A forceful side to side movement of the flukes while the whale is lying upright at the surface. The movement of the flukes is controlled by a lateral bending of the caudal peduncle.

D. TAIL SWISH: A rapid movement of the tail flukes in a dorsal-ventral direction while the whale is lying on its side. The motion is more forceful than the movement of the flukes associated with swimming while lying sideways in the water, and generally creates considerable turmoil in the water (right).

E. TAIL SLAP: A forceful slapping of the flukes against the surface of the water. This is carried out while the whale is lying either dorsal up or ventral up in the water. In order to maintain stability, the whale extends its pectoral fins straight out to either side, just below the surface. With its head completely underwater, it raises its peduncle and flukes as high up out of the water as it can, and then smashes them straight down, creating an explosion of water and sound (left).

F. PEDUNCLE SLAP: A highly aggressive behavior in which the rear portion of the body, including the caudal peduncle and the flukes, is thrown up out of the water and then brought down sideways, either on the surface of the water or on top of another whale. This constitutes one of the most intensive forms of aggression in humpback whales.

FULL BODY DISPLAYS

A. BREACH: A spectacular display in which the whale propels itself out of the water, generally clearing the surface with two-thirds of its body or more. As the whale rises above the water, it throws one pectoral fin out to the side and turns in the air about its longitudinal axis. The re-entry splash from a breach is spectacular and rather characteristic, being comprised of two distinct parts. A relatively widespread explosion of water is created as the whale hits the surface. As the force of landing carries the whale beneath the water, a second geyser-like plume of water rises up within the middle of the primary explosion.

CHAPTER NINETEEN

Interpreting Behaviors

In attempting to interpret the significance of a given behavioral display, it is important to bear three considerations in mind. First, one must be cautious in generalizing across species, especially when the degree of evolutionary relatedness is as unclear as it is, for example, between the toothed and the baleen whales. Second, given the high energy and degree of complexity involved in many of the behaviors, one must recognize the possibility that they are likely to serve a variety of functions. The particular "meaning" of a behavioral display must be cast in terms of the context in which it occurs, and one must be prepared to reinterpret the behavior as the context changes.

The third caveat to be considered is that behaviors may be interpreted at a variety of levels. That is, we may ask why a whale breaches from the viewpoint of how that behavior evolved from related species that lived earlier in evolutionary time, or we might wonder how the behavior allows the species to deal more effectively with the pressures of its current environment. **Evolution** and **adaptation** have been the "ultimate" causal explanations traditionally sought by biologists and ethologists interested in establishing the effect of environmental pressures on behavioral development across the millennia of evolutionary change.

The significance of a behavior from the "proximate" point of view is also important. In the life of a given animal, we might ask how a behavior develops **ontogenetically,** that is, how and when the behavior appears as the animal "grows up." With a much more direct explanation in mind, we might even ask what immediate **environmental** incident triggered a given response. These proximate explanations have been most

Calves engage in many high energy behaviors which appear to be play but are undoubtedly related to adult behaviors.

often sought by comparative psychologists, interested in understanding behavior in the context of its flexibility and dependence on learning. Today's scientists interested in the general field of animal behavior attempt to qualify their hypotheses about behavior by casting them in the context of the type of explanation they are hoping to achieve.

The behaviors that are described have been observed during many hundreds of hours of observations in our own research activities, and have been reported in the scientific literature by other researchers. We have observed all of these behaviors either from shore stations, from aircraft, from boats or from underwater.

Not all behaviors occur with equal frequency, nor are they produced by all segments of the population. The aggressive displays appear most frequently among competing males. Calves produce most, but not all of the behaviors described. We often see calves engaging in what appear to be imitative behaviors, and we have observed many immature attempts to produce adult forms of behaviors such as tail slaps and spy hops. While it is appropriate to refer to many of the calf activities as "play" behavior, it should be born in mind that play is not just random activity, but "practice" of those behaviors which will become more important as the calf matures.

While many of the behaviors can be seen easily from the deck of a whalewatching boat, a lot of the underwater behaviors may only be seen by the reader in photographs or film. It is not to be expected every time a whale is seen from a boat that it will immediately put on a display of spectacular behaviors; often you will see nothing more than an occasional blow. It takes a great deal of time, energy and patience to see the wide range of behaviors that we have described.

In the remainder of this chapter we will describe the general contexts in which behaviors defined in the Behavior Key may be seen to occur. While the described behaviors can be clearly defined as discrete units, in reality they occur as parts of sequences in which important functions are met. Single behaviors seldom stand on their own and take on added meaning when considered as part of more extended interactions between whales or between the whale and its environment. Most importantly, it can be seen that categories of behaviors have been developed during the process of evolution as graded means of communicating needs and intentions to other members of the species. Thus the various head behaviors can be roughly categorized in at least two ways; visual scanning and aggressive display. Similarly, respiration behaviors when considered as a group also demonstrate the potential for graded elaboration of behavioral states. Tail, pectoral fin, and breach displays provide the animal a series of alternative ways to make its presence and perhaps intentions clear to others.

It should be noted that many of the behaviors we describe are those which have been most obvious to us because they occur above the water's surface. Such behaviors constitute only a portion of the whale's activity. In fact, since it is unclear how much of the above surface behaviors are even perceived by other whales, their overall significance remains in question. One could argue that all surface behaviors are simply different ways to make noise. We think that this is highly unlikely, since the various behaviors do consistently occur in specific contexts. A more plausible argument is that surface behaviors simply reflect the end-points of underwater activities which have greater significance for the animal. To the degree that this is true, however, one must recognize that changes in surface behaviors are at least correlated with changes in underwater behaviors. Given this perspective we now describe in rather broad terms the contexts in which various behaviors, visible from the surface, occur.

Many of the head displays that we see appear to serve an orientation and/or scanning function. On those occasions where the head is brought above the surface of the water with the mouth deflated and often with the eye exposed, there is good reason to believe the whale may be visually scanning the surface of the water. Behaviors such as **spy-hops** and **head rises** have been observed in a variety of cetacean species, including orcas, bottlenose dolphins, right whales and gray whales.

The cetacean eye is well suited for in-air vision (see page 45) as well as for underwater vision, and it would be reasonable to expect that such ability would be used to advantage.

Humpbacks will increase their apparent size, perhaps to appear more menacing, by engorging their mouth with water and air.

Head displays also seem to be important in competitive encounters. Humpback whales have a wide repertoire of behaviors which can be used to signal aggression. The sight of one humpback coming head first out of the water and hurling itself down onto the back of another leaves little doubt as to the nature of the interaction. Not all aggressive behavior is so obvious. There are a variety of displays which vary along a continuum of intensity signaling increasing levels of aggression. These include **throat distension** and **head shaking** as low level displays, **jaw claps** and **inflated head lunges** as medium level displays, and **head slaps** and **butting** as more intense activities. Like many other species, a humpback appears to be able to warn intruding whales, or perhaps bluff them into thinking that it is bigger and more dominant than they are. For example, in distending the throat grooves by filling the mouth with water or air, the whales apparent size increases considerably. If that doesn't work, then there are techniques for feigning attack. Finally, should all else fail, the head or other parts of the body can be employed as full fledged weapons to drive the intruder away.

Aggressive displays may also involve a variety of respiratory behaviors. **Underwater blows** are both noisy and highly visible, at least within a whale-length or two of the animal carrying out the behavior. These exhalations may result from a kind of hyperventilation on the whale's part, or allow the whale to breathe more quickly and resume its underwater activities. At the same time, however, they provide considerable information on the location, activity and general state of the whale emitting the underwater blow.

The creation of **bubble trails** is a frequent activity among groups of whales competing to get close to a female. We have seen from aerial observations that the bubble trail is most often laid by one of the lead whales, and therefore highly visible to

Competition among male whales for access to females often turns into an intense shoving match. As two whales surface and blow simultaneously, the male on the right attempts to displace the one on the left keeping it away from the female, not shown (OPPOSITE PAGE, TOP). In an attempt to display dominance, the whale on the right uses its pectoral fin to restrain the competitor's caudal peduncle (CENTER AND BOTTOM). As the whales dive (ABOVE), the male on the left retaliates with an explosive tail slash.

BELOW: A female signals her unwillingness to be escorted by an approaching male by directing a peduncle slap towards his head.

After filling its mouth with air at the surface, the whale may release it underwater creating a cloud or a stream of bubbles.

any following whales. These bubble trails may be an attempt to create a visual screen, or they may serve a more direct communicative function—signaling anger or distress on the part of the bubbling whale. We know that bubble screens are sometimes created around divers and small boats; perhaps the bubble trail is essentially a long, drawn out bubble screen created by a whale on the move.

Another series of aggressive behaviors involves the tail, the powerful 15-ft wide flukes that serve as the whale's primary mechanism of propulsion. Whalers, and scientists interested in whale behavior, have long been aware of the power of the fluke and its potential for aggressive use. Many exciting scrimshaw scenes of the hunt for sperm whales illustrate the hapless consequence of finding one's boat within range of the flailing flukes of a wounded whale. The gray whale earned itself the name of "devilfish" among whalers, due to its ferocity when harpooned. Dolphins, as well, are quite capable of severly injuring a conspecific, or unwanted intruders such as sharks or even humans, with a slash of the flukes. Humpback whales have also been observed driving away orcas by lashing out with their flukes.

We have observed whales positioning themselves so as to present the posterior portion of their body toward an approaching whale, and sometimes toward an approaching boat. If the approaching object changes its direction to circle the whale, the animal will reposition itself to keep its tail pointed toward the intruder. In doing so, it appears to have the flukes pointed straight down below the water, with the peduncle raised slightly above, but parallel to the water's surface. When the whale is at the surface, the **tail cock** looks much like a slingshot about to be released. A similar positioning

A subadult or young whale demonstrates the power of its flukes by slapping them forcefully on the surface of the water.

of the flukes has been observed in whales swimming beneath the surface, but in this case, it seems to be associated with a moving whale slowing down.

Other fluke displays that appear to include an aggressive component are the **tail slash** and the **tail slap.** The tail slash looks like a karate chop with the fluke. The whale turns the posterior portion of its body toward a whale or intruder, and slashes its flukes back and forth, while remaining in an upright position, usually with its head lower in the water than its flukes. The tail slap may be carried out in either an upright or inverted position. In either case, the whale positions itself with its pectoral fins

Although once claimed to be a mating position, our observations have made it clear that belly to belly contact between whales is more likely to be a form of male-male competition. Here two whales rise belly to belly above the surface of the water while each attempts to topple the other. As one whale falls to the side, the bloodied jaw plate of the second gives evidence of its use as a weapon.

Hurling the rear half of its body sideways out of the water, a humpback whale becomes a formidable opponent.

stretched out to either side, in order to prevent itself from rolling over, and then lifts its flukes above the water's surface. Often one can see clearly half of the whale's body rising up out of the water. Once the flukes have reached the peak of their ascent, they are immediately brought flat down onto the water with a resounding and forceful slap that creates a very distinct explosion of whitewater. Most often, the whale will engage in repeated tail slaps, a truly impressive sight. We have observed whales tail slap more than 70 times in a row, with slaps occurring as fast as we could count them. Tail slap episodes such as these are frequently initiated in the vicinity of other whales, approaching boats, and circling aircraft flying at low altitude. They are also observed when the tail slapper is alone.

Perhaps the most aggressive type of fluke display we have witnessed is one called the **peduncle slap.** The peduncle slap describes a behavior in which one whale hurls the rear half of its body up out of the water, and brings it down sideways against the water's surface or another whale.

Some of the described behaviors occur under circumstances which appear stressful, but unrelated to clearly aggressive activity. One of these we have described as **eye widening,** a term we have had to invent for lack of an already available one.

We have seen photographs and film footage of humpback whales, especially of mothers and calves, in which the whale's eye is opened unusually wide. We have observed a similar reaction in captive dolphins that have been frightened by the introduction of a new and unfamiliar object into the water, or when taken out of the water while being transported to another location.

We believe that humpback whales react with fear when approached under water by humans under certain circumstances. For example, it is not uncommon to find researchers or photographers who get impatient in their method of approaching whales, and end up speeding in front of them in order to jump in the water and take photographs as the whales swim past the boat. Such a technique can cause the whale considerable fright.

In conjunction with eye widening in humpbacks, we have noted the occurrence of bubbles streaming from the blowholes, sudden and intense beating of the flukes, and rapid diving. All of this leads us to conclude that eye widening and some forms of bubbling indicate fear and/or general stress.

Undoubtedly, the most exciting and spectacular behavioral display in which humpback whales engage is the "breach." Thirty or more tons of whale exploding from the ocean in the flurry of a twisting breach is a breathtaking sight.

It is not entirely clear why whales breach. A variety of explanations have been proposed, for the behavior is seen in many species of cetaceans, odontoceti and mysticeti alike. It has been suggested that humpbacks breach to signal other whales that they are nearby; to stun fish while feeding; to knock off barnacles, lice, cookie-cutter sharks, or remoras; to signal behavioral states such as fear, stress, aggression or playfulness, or simply to have a look at what is above the water's surface.

Many of these explanations seem unsatisfactory with respect to the humpback. They do not appear to feed while in Hawaii, yet breaching occurs while the whales are here. Since humpbacks have been found with up to 1,000 pounds of barnacles attached, breaching is apparently unsuccessful in dislodging such "hangers-on."

There is little evidence to indicate what kind of behavioral state might be indicated by a breach. Frequency of breaching decreases and aggression increases as the size of the pod increases. This suggests that breaching does not signal aggression within

a pod, although it might be a means of warning other whales to keep away. One might wish to infer that breaching is a play activity, but it is unclear what constitutes "play" for a humpback whale, or how one might independently measure a state of playfulness. It may be that breaching occurs when whales are stressed or fearful. There is absolutely no basis for claiming that breaching is a sign of "happiness"—in spite of the fact that observations of such activity led whalers to nickname the humpback, the "merry whale."

The possibility that whales may signal their presence by breaching is an interesting one. Certainly, a breach alerts human observers not only to the whale's presence, but its exact location. Nonetheless, it remains to be shown whether a humpback whale has the ability to detect the location of a breaching animal, as opposed to simply detecting the fact that there is one somewhere in the vicinity, on the basis of hearing the sound while underwater.

One has to wonder whether breaching is the most efficient means whereby one whale can let other whales know it is in the vicinity. Whales certainly have less energetic means of signaling their presence. Mother and calf pods display an uncanny ability of avoiding each other without breaching (although breaching does occur in mother and calf pods). Singers do not need to breach to signal their location. Even if breaching does signal presence, it is difficult to believe that in the middle of the Hawaii breeding season a whale would not also need to signal something about its identity (age, sex, general fitness, readiness to mate, etc.). It is not clear that the highly variable breach is able to provide such information.

A behavior as energy-consuming as a breach is likely to serve a variety of functions. We believe that one purpose of

With only two or three beats of its flukes the animal propels itself out of the water, twists in mid-air and then crashes to the surface on its back.

the breach is to see what is above the water's surface. We have noted that in photographs of breaching whales, the orientation of the whale is in large part determined by the presence and location of the boat from which the photographer took the picture, or other boats in the vicinity. A breaching whale most frequently breaches away from the boat, with its belly turned toward it. Such an orientation would generally put the boat in the whale's field of view, and even provide stereoscopic (two-eyed) cues to enhance distance information. Other research findings about the frequency of breaches in the vicinity of boats, the effect of changes in boat direction or engine characteristics, and the number of times a given whale breaches, suggest that whales visually scan the surface for boats they can hear but cannot visually or acoustically localize underwater. While breaching may be a general startle response, the fact that the orientation of the whale is non-random with respect to the boat suggests that the whale is actually looking for or at the vessel.

It has been claimed that whales keep their eyes closed when they breach. This is unlikely to be true. While the eyes may close during a portion of the breach, it is difficult to know whether they close completely or only partially in order to reduce the amount of light entering the eye. Dolphins in captivity will often appear to have their eyes closed, but will still respond to their trainers hand signals correctly.

The whale's eye is often open during the breach providing the possibility of aerial surveillance.

TWO BROAD CATEGORIES of activities which are important determinants of the behaviors of humpback whales in Hawaii are mating and bearing offspring. These activities occur within an intricate web of social interactions permeating all facets of the whales' life and activities while in Hawaii. The temporal and geographical patterns of whale movement, the nature and length of social relations formed, and the behaviors in which the whales engage are all products of the need to mate, calve, and rear offspring. The pursuit of these needs is shaped within patterns of socialization which begin to affect the behavior of newly born calves from their first days in Hawaii.

In this section we review characteristics of migration, distribution, pod composition and social interaction that are in large part determined by the complex rules, both biological and social, of reproduction and rearing in humpback whales.

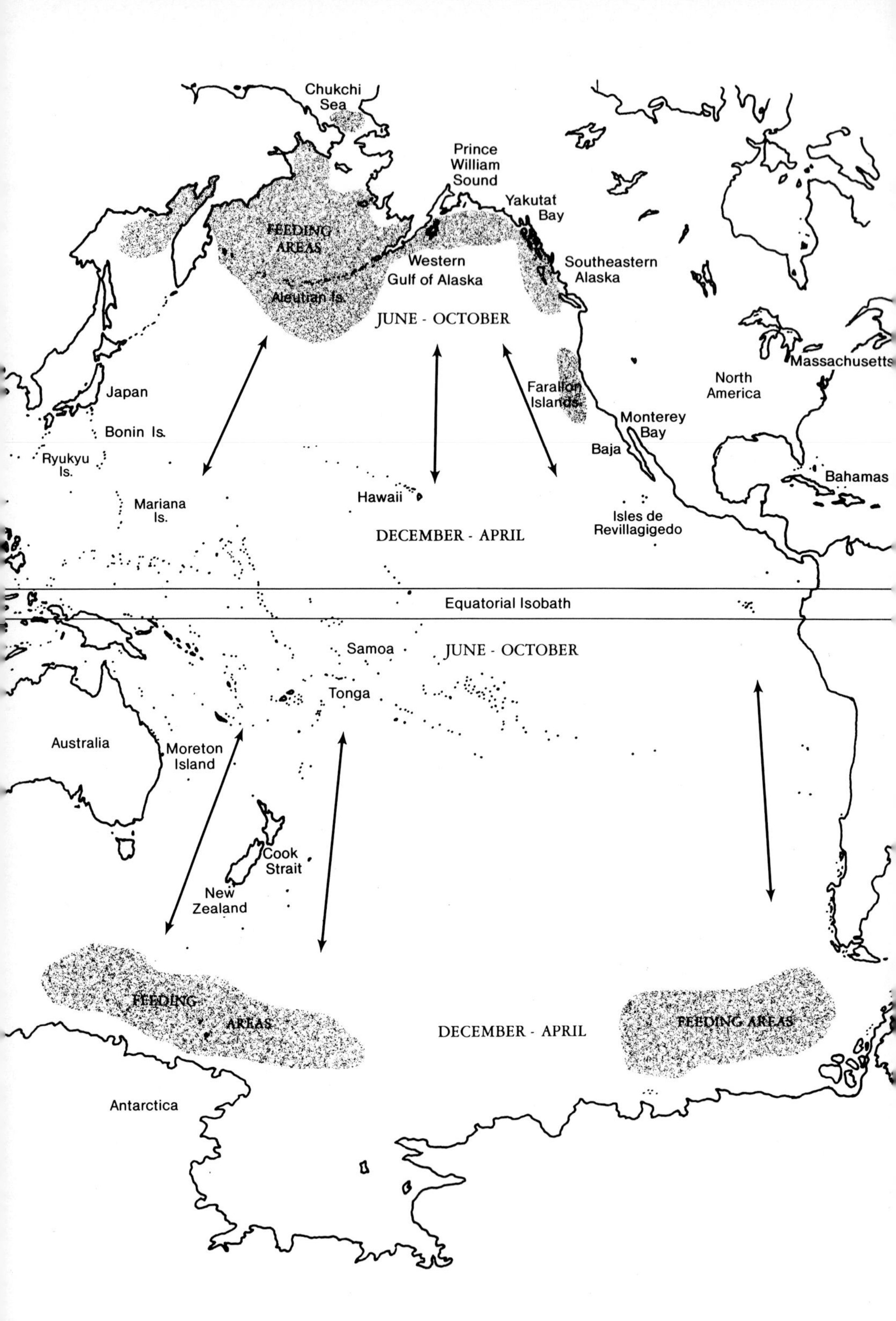

Map of the Pacific Ocean showing major feeding and breeding areas of the humpback whale. Arrows indicate general movement trends and not specific migratory routes.

CHAPTER TWENTY

Migration and Distribution

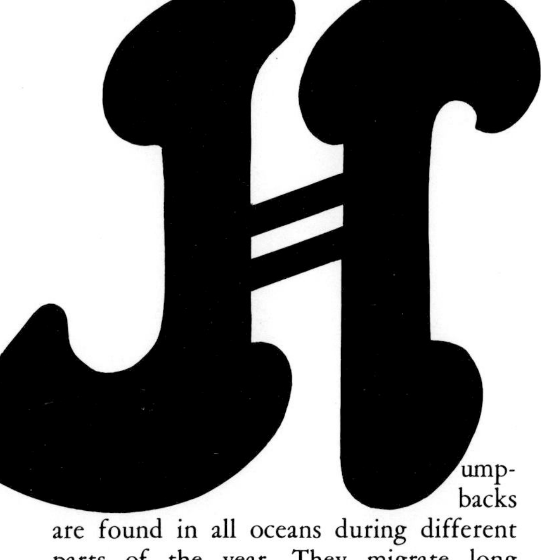

Humpbacks are found in all oceans during different parts of the year. They migrate long distances from polar waters near ice zones—rarely do they venture into the pack ice—to tropical winter breeding grounds near islands and bank areas. They tend to prefer breeding waters 75 degrees F (25 degrees C), quiet bays and leeward sides of exposed reefs with a depth of 600 feet (100 fathoms) or less, large banks wider than 2-3 miles, and water conditions relatively free of turbidity.

In the winter, North Pacific humpback whales are found in these regions: around the Bonin, Ryukyu and Mariana Islands, near Taiwan, off the coast of Baja California, the Revillagigedo and Socorro Islands off Mexico, and around the major islands of Hawaii and Kaula rock. During the summer North Pacific humpbacks are found in the nearshore waters of Southeast Alaska, and through the Aleutian Islands, into the Chukchi Sea. In the western North Pacific they range as far south as the northernmost islands of Japan. In the eastern North Pacific they are found as far south as

Monterey Bay and the Farallon Islands off the coast of Central California.

The fact that humpbacks swim south in October and north in May in both hemispheres assures the northern and southern hemisphere populations do not intermingle. Even where both populations use the same equatorial waters (10 degrees north), they are never there at the same time. Under current climatic conditions, the **equatorial isobath** forms a real biological barrier.

North Pacific humpbacks exhibit a complex pattern of migratory movements. Four summer feeding locations of the Hawaiian humpbacks lie predominantly in a north-northwesterly band stretching from southeastern Alaska, to Yakutat Bay, Prince William Sound and the western Gulf of Alaska. Research suggests that the humpbacks mix on the breeding grounds in Hawaii, but segregate in each of these four regions in summer. The majority of the humpbacks spend June through September in these waters feeding on small fish and euphausiids. Humpbacks don't feed while they are in Hawaii, although evidence from southern hemisphere humpbacks indicates that they can catch an opportunistic bite or two while transiting between breeding and feeding areas. Whalers working off east Australia at Moreton Island (26'S) reported that some of the southbound whales returning to their feeding grounds had food in their stomachs. Humpback whales in the North Pacific probably do as well.

Several hypotheses have been proposed regarding the mechanism responsible for triggering departure from the feeding grounds. These have included: decreases in water temperature, daylight, and food supply, and increases in hormonal levels associated with reproductive activity. No single factor has been found solely responsible for migratory movement, and it is more than likely dependent upon a combination of factors.

Each year those animals heading south for the winter embark on a 5,000 to 7,000 mile round-trip journey. We do not know precisely how long it takes a humpback to swim from, say, southeast Alaska to Hawaii since no whales have ever been continuously followed from one location to the other. On the basis of fluke photographs, the best migration time from Hawaii to Alaska has been computed to be 79 days, a minimum of 2800 statute miles. Of course the whale may have been in Alaskan waters for some

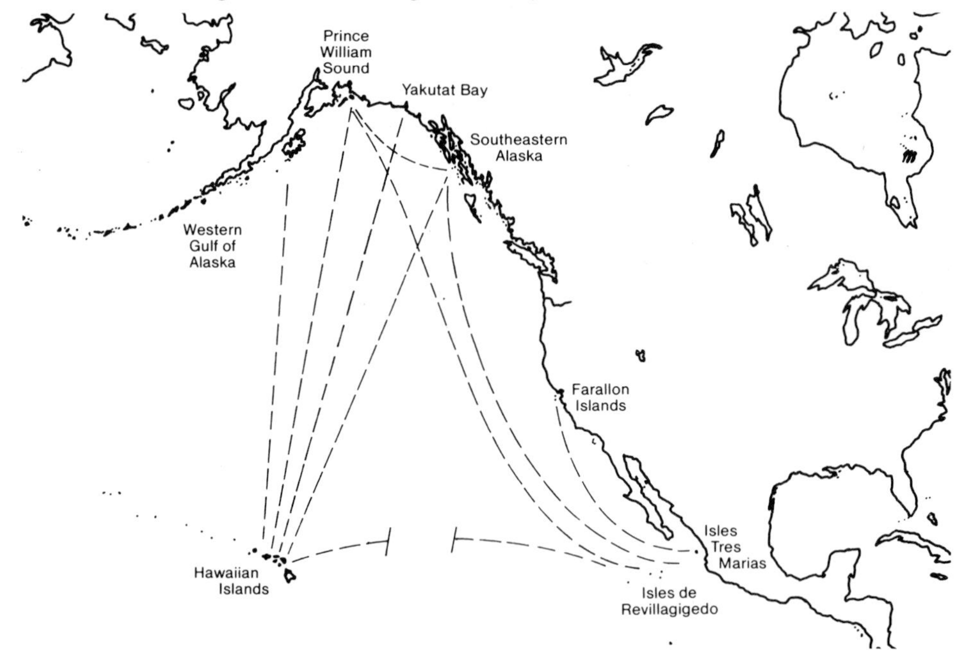

Map of the North Pacific showing patterns of resights based on photographic identification. While it is known that identified animals travelled between locations joined by dotted lines, the exact migratory routes are as yet unknown (after Baker).

Whales are seen throughout the islands and show little in the way of site specificity or regular movement patterns.

time before it was "recaptured" on film. In 1983, research on the western Atlantic stock revealed that a humpback photographically "tagged" off the Bahamas was recaptured on film 32 days later, 1,500 miles to the north, feeding on Stellwagen Banks, off Massachusetts. In 1960, while using Discovery Tags, scientists tagged an animal off Cook Strait, New Zealand and recovered the tag 20 days later when the whale was killed off Moreton Island, Australia. This animal swam 1,550 nautical miles or an average speed of just over 3 mph.

Swimming rates appear to be slow but constant, with very little milling about observed. It is generally believed that migrating whales continue to swim throughout the night.

Some whales do not leave the feeding grounds come wintertime, and move south only far enough to stay away from the pack ice which can entrap and kill humpbacks. Present knowledge about this group of whales is sketchy at best, although some findings suggest that these animals are either sexually immature or very old, non-reproductive whales.

On the basis of data collected at shore whaling stations in Australia during the 1950s and '60s, zoologist William Dawbin suggested that whales of different ages and sex arrive on the wintering grounds at different times. First to arrive are last year's mothers with their yearling calves, which will be weaned during the winter sojourn. Subadult whales of both sexes arrive next; these are not yet mature enough to be part of the active breeding population. Next to arrive are the mature males and females. Late pregnant females arrive last.

Pregnant females remain longer on the feeding grounds since they need to store as much food energy as possible—not only for the journey to the breeding grounds, but to help them survive the trauma of birth, nursing and rearing of their young.

Individuals within the different groups may arrive throughout the season, one category intermingled with the next. Peak numbers of each category appear to occur, one after the other, within about a week of each other.

On the basis of photographs and observations collected during aerial surveys of the channel areas around Molokai, Lanai, Maui and Kahoolawe in 1985, we have been able to confirm the early appearance of subadult whales, many the size of yearlings. These smaller whales, from 20-30 feet, comprise about 10% of the whales seen overall. More than half of them were seen during January and early February. Thereafter, subadults were only infrequently seen, while the number of calves observed increased from the middle of the season through the end of April. Consistent with the results of aerial surveys conducted by the University of Hawaii between 1977 and 1980, we found that early in January only about 10% of the total whales to be seen in Hawaii during the season had arrived. Rapid increase in the number of whales seen continued during February; thereafter sightings dropped off at about the same rate they had increased, until very few whales were seen toward the end of April.

Thus the pattern in Hawaii seems in large part similar to that described by Dawbin for South Pacific humpbacks.

First to head northward from the winter breeding grounds are newly pregnant females, followed by immature whales of both sexes, then the mature males and females. Mothers with newborn calves stay longest so that the calves will have time to develop a thicker layer of blubber for protection against the cold feeding waters they will soon be visiting for the first time. This segregated arrival and dispersal helps to insure survival of the species by making it possible for humpbacks to achieve maximum feeding benefit from increased food resources in polar waters during the summer.

The ability to make this long and complex migration each year demonstrates an impressive capacity for pelagic navigation. Locating the small isolated volcanic islands of Hawaii each winter and returning to the feeding regions each summer requires the use of a variety of environmental clues and sensory capabilities. In addition to acoustical orientation and sensitivity to water and temperature currents, recent studies suggest that navigation may depend upon a system designed to detect changes in the earth's magnetic field. Humpbacks may "home in" on their breeding and feeding grounds with the help of a metaloid substance, **magnetite,** found near the frontal lobe of their brains. Recent evidence on strandings indicates that beached whales that appear outwardly healthy may suffer from disorientation due to electrical storms high in the earth's atmosphere which create distortions in the magnetic field (see Strandings, pg. 159).

Whatever their secret of pathfinding, humpbacks regularly appear in Hawaiian waters in mid-November. The whales do not arrive "en masse" but flow in and out of the islands throughout the period from November through May, although some stragglers may be reported as late as July.

There has been little success in finding predictable patterns of movement by the whales across the season, although extensive shore-based observations have been carried out on the Big Island of Hawaii, on Maui and on Molokai.

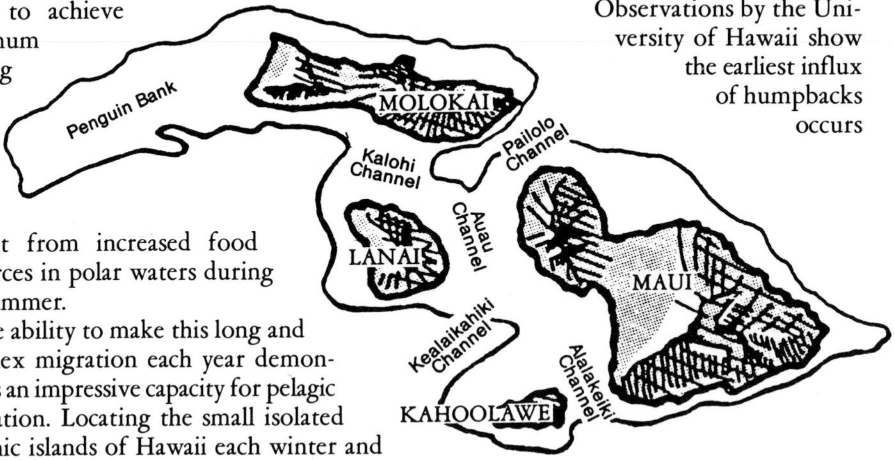

Observations by the University of Hawaii show the earliest influx of humpbacks occurs around the Big Island, followed by large numbers of whales two or three weeks thereafter in the channel between Maui, Lanai, Molokai and around Kauai. We believe that Pailolo Channel, between Maui and Molokai, may be an important "highway" into the waters of the so-called Four-Island Region—pods as large as 22 whales have been seen in Pailolo early in the season. And yet, interestingly, shore-spotting data from Maui's southwest coast indicate that whales do not move in a pattern consistent with a continuous flow of whales in a northwesterly direction.

CHAPTER TWENTY ONE

Social Dynamics

While the humpbacks are in Hawaii, they appear to show little site fidelity, either within or across years. They do not appear to form stable groups, with the exception of the mother and calf. We do find a variety of pod types, but it is important to note that calling a given group of whales a pod does not necessarily mean that interaction may not be taking place between that group and another whale or group of whales at some distance away. We simply do not know what the effective range of communication for humpback whales is. In any case, it is apparent from both boat and shore-based observations, that interchange occurs between the various pods of whales that are seen moving about the islands.

In general, the most frequent pod size that is seen is 2 - 3 animals. The next most frequent pod size is the "singleton," or lone whale. While it is not uncommon to find pods ranging in size from 4 - 8 whales, these larger groups are seen much less

frequently than pods of 1, 2 or 3 whales. We have, however, encountered on rare occasions pods of more than 20 whales. The various pod sizes seem to be dependent upon the activities in which the whales are engaged, such as weaning, courting, mating, fighting, nursing, singing, resting, playing, and just plain swimming.

Single whales are generally considered to be males, an idea originally based on the findings of Japanese whaling data. Later, it was shown that in Hawaii and in the Caribbean (where most North Atlantic humpbacks migrate in the winter) so-called "singing whales" were almost always found alone. This suggests that singing is a male behavior, most likely associated with mating activity (since singing has been found predominantly, but not solely in the winter assembly areas). It was not until 1979, however, that a number of lone singers in Hawaii were photographed. Using a technique perfected by Deborah Glockner, researchers were able to determine that the whales photographed were males. All sexually identified singing whales in Hawaii have been found to be males.

It is believed that by singing, male humpbacks may advertise their fitness and willingness to mate, perhaps attracting females, keeping competing males away, or both. Singing singletons remain in the same general location for extended periods. They surface at quite regular intervals. A given whale will maintain a very predictable "down-time," although across singers the range of intervals varies between 12 - 20 minutes. After surfacing, the whale will blow two or three times, generally dive with flukes up, and continue singing. Singers will stop singing if another whale approaches, or if they approach another whale or pod of whales. Singing whales usually maintain a separation of some two or three miles from each other. The space between singers seems more important than the location of the singing itself, for singers are found to range over a variety of locations during the season.

Pods of two whales may include two adults, two subadults, an adult and subadult, a mother and yearling, or a mother and calf. The frequency of two-whale pods decreases across the season. This may reflect the successful weaning of a yearling, which may then join with other immature whales; or may result from the birth of a calf. If pregnant females tend to travel in the company of another whale, it may suggest that humpbacks form larger aggregations prior to leaving the islands for Alaska. With the exception of the mother-calf pair, pods of two whales do not appear to be characterized by any unique behavior patterns, except that they tend to be rather boring animals to watch. It has been shown that the relative frequency and variety of behaviors increase as pod size increases.

Large pods of whales generally engage in a variety of aggressive activities believed associated with competition for mates. These pods are seen infrequently and remain together for only brief periods of time. Often they contain a calf, never more than one, and sometimes one or more subadult whales. Perhaps because of the high percentage of conspicuous activities found in these large pods, they are often found accompanied by a variety of other cetaceans. These have included bottlenose, spinner, spotted, and rough-toothed dolphins, false killer and pilot whales, and even on one occasion a northern right whale.

Humpback whales are often accompanied by other cetaceans such as the bottlenose dolphin in the above photo.

CHAPTER TWENTY TWO

Calving

It is generally believed that humpback calves are both conceived and born in Hawaii. Data collected by biologists working aboard whaling ships revealed that ovulation in females, and increased testis weight and spermatogenesis count in males, peak during the winter months. Additionally, it has been found that the gestation period for humpbacks is 10 - 12 months. Starting around the end of January, sightings of calves are quite common. The rather surprising fact, however, is that there is no well-documented evidence of an actual birth in Hawaiian waters. While many claim to have witnessed a birth, it is found on closer examination that the observer *thought* they saw a newly born calf. Two anecdotal reports of witnessing parturition have been reported. In one case, a charter boat operator reported getting into the water to help a female in distress with a still-born calf partially emerged from, but apparently stuck in the birth canal. In the second case, a commercial sport diver from Lanai reported filming a full birth underwater (unfortunately the murkiness of the water was too great to identify what is happening in the film).

It is possible that many calves are born while the mothers are still enroute to Hawaii, although we have seen a number of obviously pregnant whales from both the air and underwater. It may also be that births generally occur at night. Whatever the timing, a humpback whale mother in late pregnancy selects a relatively shallow, usually inshore area where she and her newborn offspring will be free from harassment by preying sharks, sexually active males, and unpredictable boats. Whalers have reported that newborn calves are almost white in color and darken within hours of birth. We have observed such calves on a number of occasions (see photo page 25).

After the calf is born, the mother remains close to shore during some number of hours of post-parturition recovery. While there are many popular beliefs concerning the need for the mother to lift the calf up to the surface to breathe, or for the mother to repeatedly breach in order to snap the umbilical cord, it seems inappropriate to speculate on the actual parturition sequence without benefit of well-documented evidence. The contention that the calf is born inshore, in an isolated spot, with the mother pretty much on her own is supported by the circumstances in which light colored, small and relatively inactive calfs have been found in the company of mothers resting at the surface for extended periods.

Following a period of perhaps a week, during which the mother and calf remain in near-shore waters, they extend their range of travel to include deeper water, within two to three miles of shore. As they do so, they frequently either join, or are joined by a third whale. This **escort** whale is generally assumed to be a sexually active male. The escort whale does not remain with the mother and calf for more than a day at most, with most associations lasting for only a couple of hours, or in many cases, only a few minutes.

Frequently, the escort whale will leave the mother and calf if a boat approaches, while on other occasions, it will carry out defensive maneuvers such as positioning itself between the mother and calf and the

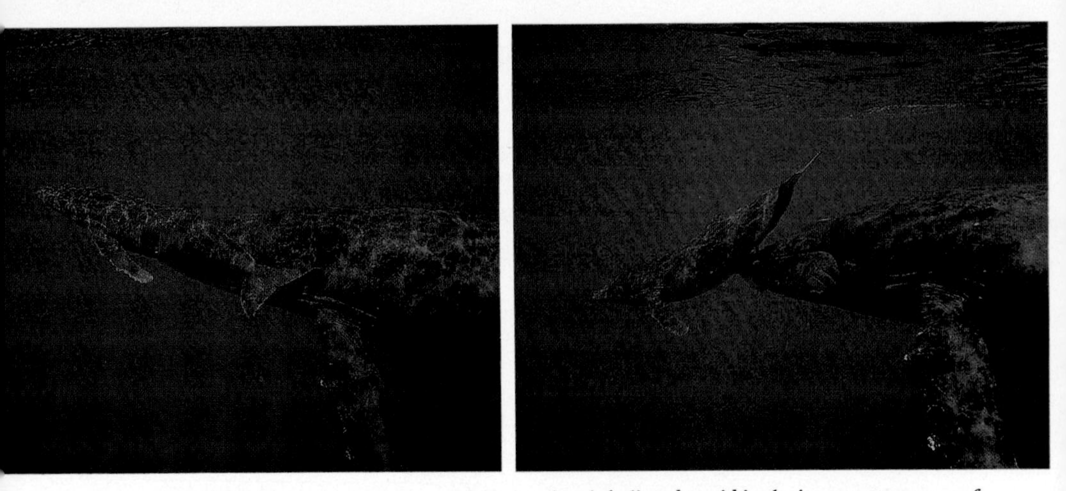

The close contact in which mothers are seen with their calves is believed to aid in the important process of bonding and attachment between the new mother and her infant offspring.

approaching boat. When there are divers in the water, the escort may also interpose itself, or create a visual screen by blowing bubbles out of its blowholes. The escort may even threaten a boat or diver with its flukes. Once while we were swimming next to and photographing a mother and calf, an escort whale suddenly appeared 60 feet below, heading directly toward us at high speed. We knew that escorts often interpose themselves between the mother-calf pair and intruding whales, boats or divers. Since it was not readily apparent, however, how 40 tons of escort was going to fit within the 15 feet of space between us and the mother and calf, we held our breath and waited for what was quickly shaping up to be our last encounter with a humpback whale! To our relief and surprise the escort stopped about 20 feet below us, turned slightly on its side to expose one ominously bulging eye, and began blowing a stream of

Calves are frequently very curious; we have been approached closely while in small boats as well as during underwater observations. From birth, the calf moves about with alertness and coordination.

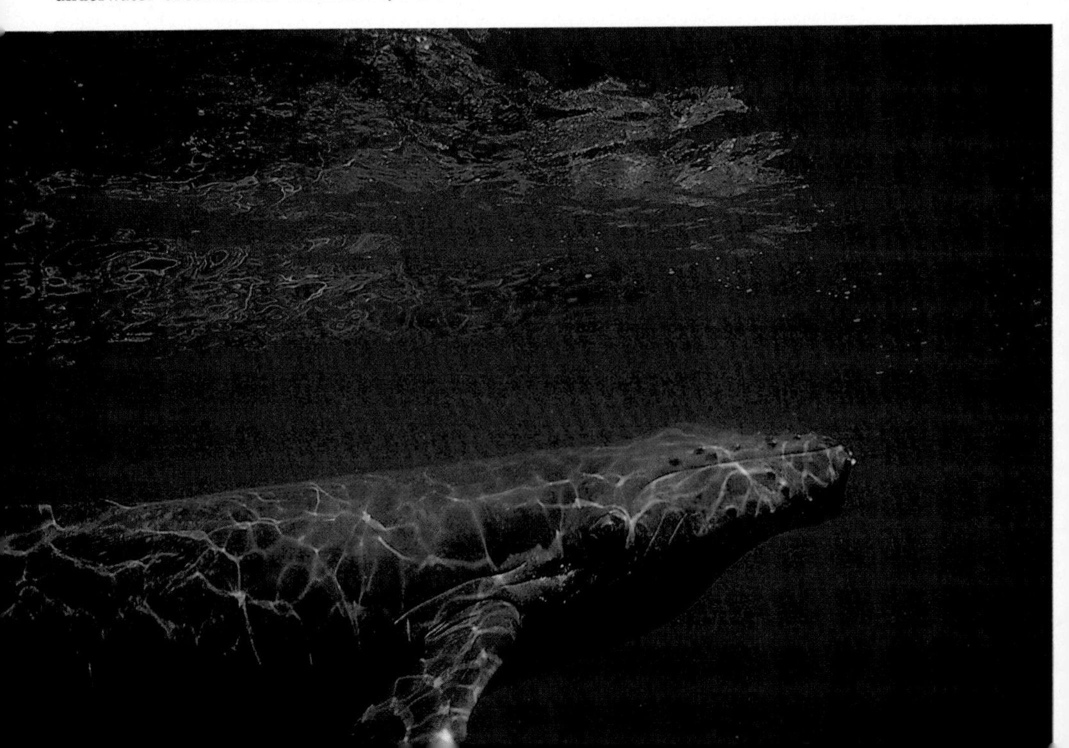

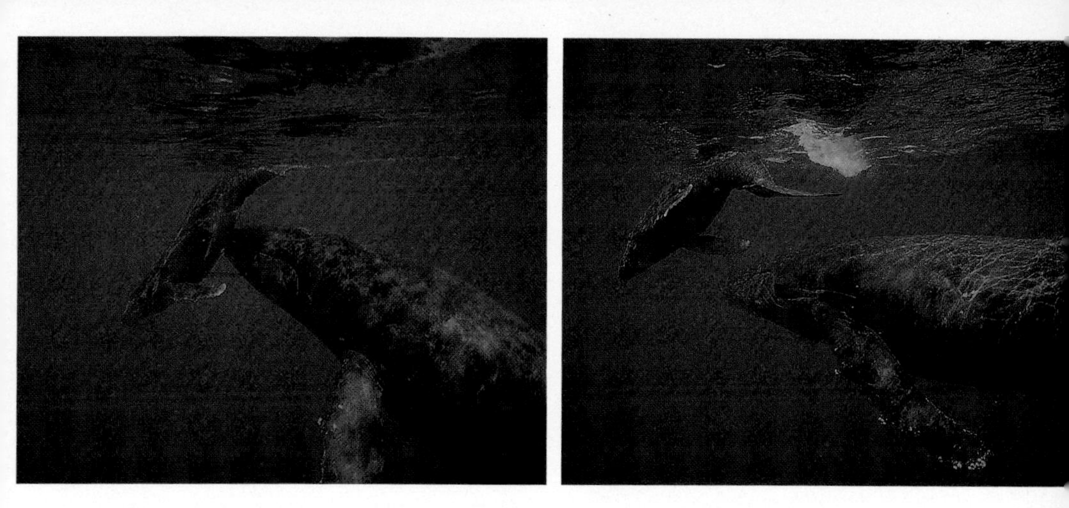

bubbles. As the bubbles rose to the surface, they struck our body and swim fins and immediately changed into a fine screen of smaller bubbles that completely enshrouded us, blocking our vision. When we regained our badly fractured composure and swam out of the bubble screen, the mother, calf and escort were nowhere to be seen!

When a mother and calf are joined by other whales, there is generally a considerable increase in the amount and intensity of above-surface activity associated with highly aggressive attempts by the new arrivals to keep one another away from the mother and calf. It is now generally accepted that these groups of three to six or more whales chasing after mothers and calves are comprised primarily of males, attempting to displace each other, remain with the mother, and perhaps win the opportunity to mate with her.

Data collected from whaling ships

Mothers and calves are often seen in shallow waters of 25 fathoms (150 feet) or less. This pair is seen gliding over a reef in 60 feet of water.

Swimming on its back just below the water's surface, this yearling displays the nearly "set" pigmentation pattern on the ventral side of the flukes.

indicated some small number of females (perhaps 10% or fewer) undergo **post-partum ovulation.** That is to say, even though **lactating** (producing milk), the female whale is still able to be impregnated. In heavily-exploited groups such as the North Pacific humpback, it may be that the incidence of post-partum ovulations has increased as an adaptive response to the threat of extinction. The ability to undergo a number of ovulations within the season would also enable the mother to replace a still-born or defective calf by becoming pregnant again. These factors in all probability make it well worth a male's time to seek out and court females even when they are accompanied by a suckling calf.

At birth, the calf is what one might consider **precocial,** that is, fully able to move about on its own, with all senses alert and functional. While it is possible that the calf may initially be in danger of sinking to the bottom, it is unclear whether or not the mother must in all cases lift her calf to the surface to breathe.

It is certainly the case that the mother will engage in a great deal of contactual behavior, but this may be more for the purpose of insuring that the calf stays nearby. Using her head and pectoral fins, the mother can be seen nudging, corraling and coaxing her calf to stay close by as they move along.

The characteristic position for the calf is just above and to one side of the mother's head when they are underway. In this fashion, the calf is always able to maintain visual contact with its mother. During the first few days after birth, it is likely necessary that the relationship between the mother and calf be directed primarily toward establishing a very powerful bond, so that the mother will recognize and remain close to her calf, and the system of communicative contact and vocalizations will be understood and attended to by the calf.

The calf begins to nurse soon after birth. The mother has two nipples, located on either side of the vaginal slit on her ventral surface, between the umbilicus ("belly-button") and the anus. The nipples are connected to the lobes of the mammary glands, which are long and oval-shaped, and lie between the blubber and the musculature

Newborn calves surface to breathe approximately every 3 - 5 minutes. Mothers will typically surface every 10 - 15 minutes, always in close proximity to the calf.

of the abdomen. In humpback whales, the mammary glands of a mature female may be as large as 7 feet long and 2 feet wide. During lactation, they go from a thickness of about 2 inches, to as thick as one foot, and the nipples, or teats, protrude through the expanded mammary slits. After finding the nipple, the calf takes it in its mouth, and curls its tongue around it. Interestingly, the calf does not so much suckle as receive the milk that is squirted under pressure into its mouth. Apparently, the stimulation of the nipple by the calf results in a reflexive ejaculation of the milk by the mother.

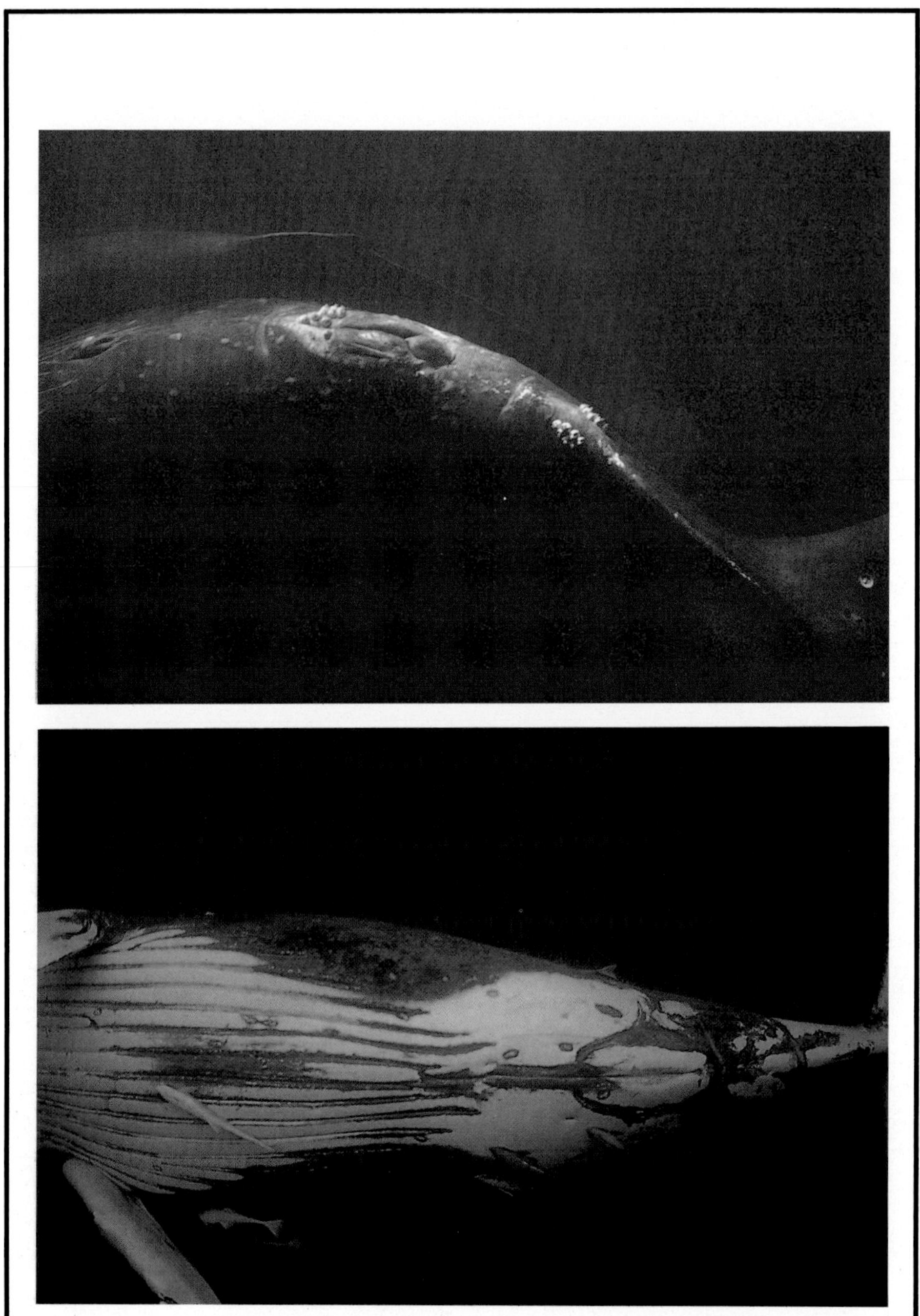

The female (top) shows the characteristic hemispherical lobe on the posterior edge of the genital opening, missing in the photograph of the male (bottom). Also visible in the top photo are the mammary slits, on either side of the genital opening. (See also page 71.)

Whales' milk is much more viscous, or thick, than the milk of terrestrial mammals. It has less water than the milk of other mammals (40-50% for the humpback versus 80-90% for many domestic animals), much more fat (40-50% as compared with 2-17%), and about twice the concentration of protein. Approximately 100-130 gallons are produced per day. The highly-concentrated, prolific quantities of milk permit the calf to grow at the rate of nearly a foot per month. The newborn humpback, approximately 12 feet in length and weighing upwards of two tons, will double its overall length within a year.

When one considers the fact that the mother provides her calf with such enormous quantities of food, while apparently not feeding herself during the initial two to three months of the calf's life, one can see that the mother must recognize and feed only her own calf. It is also important that she not waste her resources on a calf which shows any indication of not being able to survive. In keeping with such expectations, it has been repeatedly observed that not more than one calf is found within a pod. On perhaps two or three occasions, researchers have reported exceptions to this finding, but it is very possible that they were observing a calf and yearling. These observers may possibly have seen twin calves, but this is highly unlikely. The well-known illustration by Charles Scammon, a famous whaling captain of the 19th century, which shows twin calves nursing from their mother is an example of artistic license.

Nursing consists of frequent episodes of short duration, perhaps limited by the calf's ability to hold its breath and remain underwater. It does not seem that the mother nurses the calf while they are both traveling, either at the surface or beneath the water. Neither have anecdotal reports of a mother lying on her side at the surface while a calf nurses been corroborated.

While it is generally accepted that a calf seen underneath its mother, with its head at her genital area, is most likely nursing—we know of only two cases in which the observ-

Newborn calves use their long, flexible pectoral fins, and powerful flukes to propel themselves with apparent ease in graceful lines of speed and power, as they move beneath the seas.

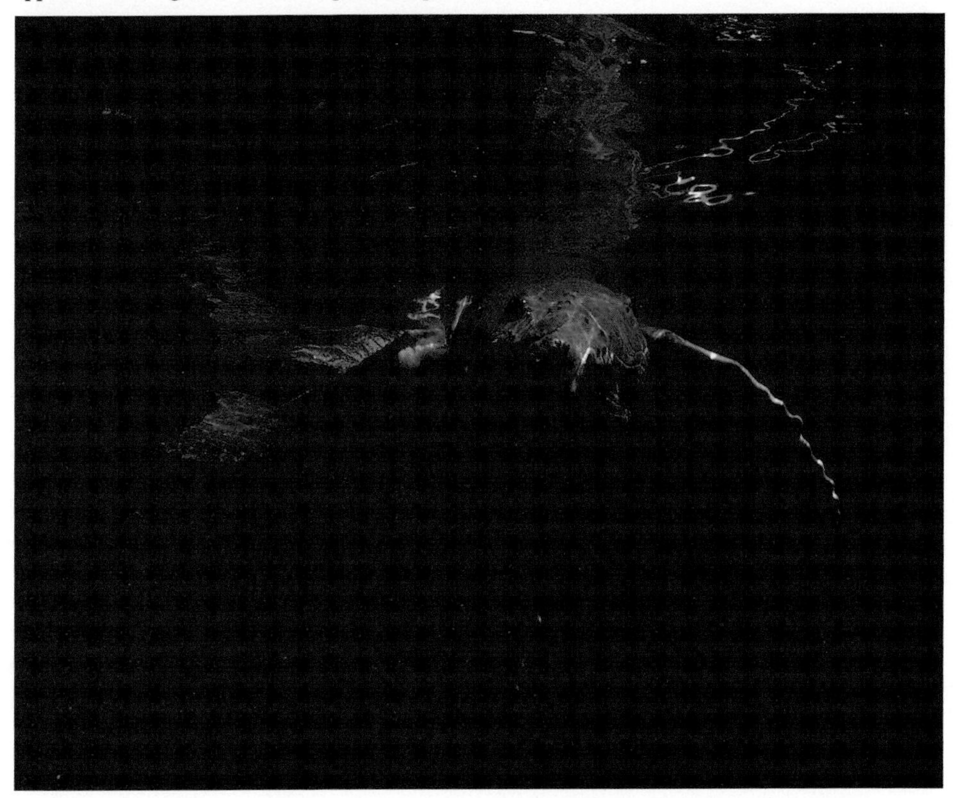

er actually was able to establish that nursing was definitely taking place. In each case the diver was able to see a whitish cloud briefly suspended by the mother's genitals when the calf pulled its head away.

Lactation is believed to continue for 8–12 months. Weaning begins in earnest during the mother's return to Hawaiian waters at the end of the calf's first year, and is complete by the time they arrive back on the feeding grounds the following summer. During the calf's first summer with its mother in the colder, food-rich waters of the north, some ingestion of small fish or euphausiids may occur. In southeast Alaska, during the summer months, one can watch mothers and their calves as they search about for food. It is an amusing sight to witness the antics of the calf as it accompanies its mother during her attempts to create bubble nets around schools of prey. More often than not, it seems, the calf creates such a disturbance that one wonders how the mother is able to feed at all. We have seen a large calf alternately reappear with one of two adult whales within 300 feet of each other, at intervals of 10-15 minutes. It may well be that while the calf is with one adult, the other is able to feed.

As shown by this newborn breaching beside its mother, calves must either be born precocious or learn rapidly the behaviors they will need to accompany their mother during the long migration to the feeding grounds.

CHAPTER TWENTY THREE

Mating

Just as we have yet to document a birth, we have yet to see unequivocal evidence of mating. Since we know that the gestation period ranges between 10 - 12 months, the obvious implication is that mating occurs while the whales are in or near Hawaii. Although at least one observer has seen what the whalers used to refer to as a "pink sea snake," the impressive 3-8 foot long penis of the male, nobody has yet witnessed an actual intromission. Our conclusions about courting and mating in humpback whales depends, in large part, on what we know about similar activities in other species of baleen whales, particularly the gray whale and the right whale. Such generalizations are used only to guide us in our observations of humpback whale reproductive behavior, since the mating systems of the different species of whales vary considerably.

It is customary to think of the large baleen whales like the humpback as huge but sedate "gentle giants" quietly roaming across the world's oceans. This image is reinforced by the brief view most of us have of humpbacks, when we see small groups of two or three whales, or a mother and her calf. In actual fact, observations of large,

A head lunging escort (right foreground) interposes itself between the female (left) and an approaching male (center).

surface-active groups of whales during the breeding season provide a very different picture of the humpback's temperment. As females move through the inshore waters of the islands they are periodically accompanied by sexually mature males. It is not known whether the females selectively approach males to whom they are attracted (perhaps by the male's song), or whether the males actively search for receptive females. Once a male finds a sexually receptive female, he must work hard to keep other adult males away. Males do not appear to search in groups for females, but once a female appears, she will quickly be joined by any adult in the area, and they will begin to compete with each other for access to her. While not a fight to the death, the intensity of the competition does dispell the myth of the "gentle giant."

If the males appear unable to agree on which of them will "escort" the female (thereby increasing the likelihood of a mating opportunity) a high-speed chase begins, with the female leading the way, and all the interested males (and sometimes curious subadult whales) strung out behind. Not all of the escort whales actively engage in aggressive behavior.

The role of the female in the chase is unclear. She may be running away from the group of highly-excited males because she wants nothing to do with them, or she may be providing them the opportunity to "show their stuff" as they chase her and fight with each other. Each male attempts to remain close to the female, serving as her **primary escort,** while trying to drive the other suitors or **secondary escorts** away. Head slaps, inflated head rises, tail slaps, peduncle slaps, and head butting occur with frequency and vigor. The whale most successful in remaining near the female generally does so by carrying out a wide variety of strenous activities primarily involving the head and tail. Following a period of jostling, bumping, charge and counter-charge, the fierce competition comes to an end, with many of the presumed males dispersing (sometimes in a number of smaller groups). The primary escort may have to prove himself this way a

The males (shown above) continue to compete for access to the female by attempting to displace each other through a series of inflated head displays and head butts.

Following the competitive encounters illustrated on the previous page, one of the males successfully drives away the other, and continues to accompany the female. The previously aggressive encounters give way to courtship activity, including the pec slapping of the female, shown above.

number of times over a period of hours.

After the competition between males is complete, the female must somehow indicate her willingness to favor the attentions of the successful male. At this stage the "courting pod" consists of the primary escort interacting with the female in the presence of two or more spectator whales. It is not clear that the spectators are mandatory, but they are almost always present when what seems to be courtship activity is taking place. The two active whales engage in a great deal of body contact, including mutual pectoral fin caresses and slaps, belly-to-belly rubbing, alternate diving under one another, and a variety of forms of nuzzling with the head area. One whale will almost always be seen engaging in a great deal of pectoral fin slapping on the surface of the water, sometimes lying on one side while swimming slowly about with half of the tail exposed above the water, sometimes lying belly up, then rolling in the water while first one and then the other pectoral fin is raised high above the water and then brought splashing down onto the surface. The whale may lie belly up, raise both pectoral fins in the air, usually crossing them in the process, and then slaps both simultaneously to each side. Pectoral fin displays such as these usually involve long bouts of repetitive slaps.

The relatively slow-paced swimming that usually accompanies these displays, in conjunction with the almost total absence of threatening or aggressive tail behaviors, supports the conclusion that these are not the competitive, fierce bouts of jousting described earlier. On the other hand, if such activity were immediately preliminary to intromission, one would expect to see an erect penis somewhere in the pod, but none has appeared in the presence of such activity to date. The failure to see evidence of mating is particularly intriguing, given the rather immodest behavior of other species of mysticetes. Male right whales and gray whales may be seen rolling at the surface, waving their erect penises in the air during their courtship activities.

The role of the spectators during the period when the primary escort and the female begin to attend to each other is not clear. They may remain in the vicinity as

hopeful understudies should the female lose interest in the primary escort. They may simply be curious onlookers. If humpback whales mate promiscuously (both males and females mate repeatedly with different partners throughout the breeding season) as many researchers believe, the members of the audience may be other males or females waiting for their own opportunity. In some baleen whales, the additional whales may even help out during copulation by holding the partners in place. It may well be the case that courtship is a very protracted business, extending over days, or possibly weeks, with many false starts. We shall undoubtedly know the full story one day; in the meantime we must simply be satisfied with knowing only that mating activity is a rigorous and often aggressive pursuit for humpbacks.

Multiple escorts are also frequently seen in the company of mothers and calves. Perhaps the mother, slowed down as she is by the presence of her calf, is an attractive target for males. Mothers do not appear to always return an escort whale's interest. A possible key to the degree of readiness of the mother to be attended by an escort may be the position of the calf during the period of time the escort is present. On some occasions, the calf remains on the side of the mother opposite to the escort, with the escort trailing behind. On other occasions, the mother and escort will appear closer together than the mother and calf, and they can even be seen contacting each other with their pectoral fins, with one whale diving below the other while the calf remains close to the surface, two or three whale lengths from the adults.

When courting pods are approached by a boat, the escorts will often carry out a number of behaviors that appear very similar to the ones directed at other whales when they approach. Interpositioning, bubble screens, tail threats, inflated head rises, and underwater exhalations have all been encountered by observers in boats or in the water, on approaching courting pods. When there are highly active escorts, three or more, the boat is totally ignored if it remains at some distance. If the boat pursues, it may create havoc with the pod, causing the whales to disperse, or it may be treated to a variety of threats and defensive maneuvers. In general, the less obtrusive the boat the greater likelihood it will simply be ignored.

Captain Cook first landed in Kealakekua on the Big Island in 1776. Within 50 years American whaling ships made Hawaii a regular port-of-call.

CHAPTER TWENTY FOUR

Historical Ecology

Whales have played an important part in the cultural and economic history of the Hawaiians, but not in the way most people think. In spite of the fact that the humpback whale is, in current times, a regular and highly visible visitor to these waters, there remains a significant mystery as to how long humpbacks have been coming here. Louis Herman of the University of Hawaii, has written that there is little evidence of the humpbacks having been in Hawaiian waters more than 200 years ago. It is certainly true that various species of toothed whales, called "Palaoa" by the Hawaiians, were familiar to local inhabitants and became a part of the legends and intricate systems of taboos. But there is no evidence that baleen whales such as the humpback were ever seen. Certainly there is no evidence that the Hawaiians hunted baleen whales before the 19th century. The Hawaiians did not find the meat of whales and dolphins very tasty, so whalemeat, and therefore whalehunting, never

"Rising with his utmost velocity from the furthest depths, the Sperm Whale thus booms his entire bulk into the pure element of air, and piling up a mountain of dazzling foam, shows his place to the distance of seven miles and more. In those moments, the torn, enraged waves he shakes off, seem his mane; in some cases, this breaching is his act of defiance."
from Herman Melville, *Moby Dick.*

became an important part of their evolving culture.

Whaling ships first arrived in Hawaii during the first quarter of the 19th century when the *Balaena* from New Bedford and the *Equator* from Nantucket anchored off the Big Island in 1819. A few years later the whalers discovered that the nearshore waters off Lahaina and Honolulu were more hospitable and provided a safer anchorage. These whalers were not looking for humpback whales but were on their way to the so-called Japan Grounds, where sperm whales could be found in large numbers. Both Honolulu and Lahaina were "roadsteads," often for hundreds of ships at a time, which engaged in a wide variety of whaling and whale-related activities. On many occasions, native Hawaiians were recruited by captains desperate to replace sailors who abandoned ship, or were killed in the often wild activities that overtook the towns of Honolulu and Lahaina while the ships were in port.

Richard Dana, in his book *Two Years Before The Mast* speaks highly of the "kanaka" (Hawaiian men) sailors he met, calling them the most sensitive and trustworthy he knew, and claiming he would far quicker approach a Hawaiian when in need than one of his own countrymen.

The presence of the whaling ships did lead to a shore-based whale fishery for about 30 years during the period of 1840-1870, and the promise of humpback whales in great numbers was used as an attempt to lure whale ships from Honolulu harbor

Between 1840 and 1870 shore-based whaling stations on Maui operated sporadically using techniques adapted from Yankee whalers. Such techniques were still in use 100 years later in the Polynesian islands of Tonga.

to Lahaina in 1856. By the late 1860s there were up to five shore-based whaling stations in operation, but success at taking humpbacks was so sporadic, that each capture was sufficient to warrant a full-blown account in the local papers. The method was to set out after a mother and calf, harpoon the calf as quickly as possible to keep the mother close by, and then attempt to lance the mother repeatedly until "the sight of thin blood and then thick blood told the story of success." The price of oil rendered from humpback blubber was much lower than the more highly regarded sperm whale oil. The humpbacks, which fast while in Hawaiian waters, generally gave little return for the effort required to bring them ashore. It is little surprise, therefore, that the shore-based whale stations were a short-lived enterprise.

Throughout the end of the 19th and beginning the 20th centuries, humpback whales in Hawaii were of little interest. Along the west coast of the mainland, and throughout much of their feeding area, however, they were hunted intensively. It is interesting that although they were brought to the very edge of extinction, nobody seemed to notice any difference in the numbers of whales which came to Hawaii in the winter. Until the mid 1970s, there were only two periods during which whales received any attention. During WWII they were used for target practice by bombers. In the 1950s, an Oahu-based whale-watch group was formed, which observed small numbers of whales in the area of Kokohead. Little notice seems to have been paid the humpbacks otherwise. All that was to change with the increased interest in studying living whales, which hit Hawaii in earnest in 1975.

CHAPTER TWENTY FIVE

Conservation

The North Pacific humpbacks have begun to show signs of recovery. Nonetheless increased demands on their habitat continue to threaten the likelihood that they will recover to former stock levels. For any animal to survive it must be able to adapt to changes in its environment, but it is difficult for humpbacks and other marine mammals to adapt when these changes literally happen overnight. The humpbacks' songs, once thought to travel thousands of miles uninterrupted, must now compete with machines that dredge, blast, drill and make war.

In Hawaii, the humpbacks are faced with increased vessel traffic, not only from the recreation and tourism sector, but also from the military and shipping lines. The whales have had to contend with ordnance detonation and military activity surrounding the island of Kahoolawe, in the very heart of their breeding grounds.

In Hawaii, humpbacks are faced with increased vessel traffic from the recreational and tourism sector, as well as from the military and shipping lines.

Growth on the land affects the marine environment as buildings usurp the coastline, erradicate the natural run-off patterns, and dump huge amounts of mud and fresh water into the ocean. With the run-off comes pesticide from agricultural areas.

Whalewatching has become a big business in the U.S., indeed, an industry. Over one million enthusiasts go whalewatching in America each year. The total revenue from all whale activities, including sales of memorabilia and memberships in whale organizations, amounts to nearly $100 million annually. When compared with killing whales, recreational whalewatching represents a low- or non-consumptive utilization of a remarkably renewable economic resource.

Coincident with the onslaught of whalewatchers in Hawaii the National Marine Fisheries Service has taken steps to enforce the terms of the Marine Mammal Protection Act and the Endangered Species Act. This has primarily taken the form

Whalewatch excursions narrated by research scientists or certified naturalists are an effective tool for educating the public about the natural history and conservation of humpback whales.

of monitoring commercial and recreational water use, surveying research results, and controlling approaches to whales by vessels, aircraft, swimmers, and divers (see page 157). There is little doubt that whales can be disturbed when recklessly approached by any vessel or aircraft. Boat operators must move with consideration around the whales. After all, Hawaii is their bedroom, and over use or misuse of the marine environment could make the whale's habitat uninhabitable.

With the protection of North Pacific humpback whales from commercial hunting in 1966, and the implementation of a worldwide moratorium on whaling in 1986, the concept of conservation and management must be examined in a new and different light. Past whale management strategies have reflected consumptive needs, for example the determination of the maximum number of whales that could be removed from a given population. Early research was based on meeting these needs. The 1970s brought with it an outraged public that was hellbent on saving the whales. Fueled by the humpbacks' curious song and spectacular underwater films the demand was made for more information, which was to be gained from living whales rather than dead. From the beginning a most curious marriage was formed, with the scientists making new and exciting discoveries, and the public eagerly awaiting each new insight.

No other scientific field, except perhaps ornithology, has attracted so many people, both professionals and amateurs. Because of the popularity of whales, many scientific findings are first published not in scientific journals, but in popular magazines allowing for a wide circle of informed and passionate observers. This has had the result of allowing the non-scientist an opportunity to satisfy his or her curiosity by supporting scientific research. Instead of a field where experts dominate the less informed, the emphasis in whale research is on a collective commitment to education, habitat protection, and scientific credibility.

Whalewatching has become a springboard for stimulating further interest in the whales, their habitat, and the value of "saving" them. For many, a whalewatching trip is their initial venture on the ocean, and provides the opportunity to experience first-hand the dependence of whales on the marine environment and to understand how essential it is that the oceans be kept clean and uncongested. In the words of sociobiologist Stephanie Kaza: "The power of this experience should not be underestimated: through cetacean education there is an avenue for counteracting the tendency toward self-destruction that dominates world politics and human relationships today. With whales and dolphins, we begin to observe the natural order of life and validate our own experiences of that which we hold in common."

Will the humpbacks ever leave Hawaii? That is a particularly difficult question to answer. There is evidence that humpbacks in other parts of the world have moved out of areas where food availability, or whaling and maritime activities, have threatened their livelihood. The many research projects carried out in Hawaiian waters along with the enforcement of the Endangered Species Act and the Marine Mammal Protection Act are important for helping us understand the needs of the whales so that we may help protect the habitat necessary for their continued existence. To ensure their survival, those of us who have an interest in the recovery of the humpback whale should become educated about their nature and habits before imposing on their life and activities, just as we might educate ourselves about the language and culture of another country before visiting it.

CHAPTER TWENTY SIX

Looking Ahead

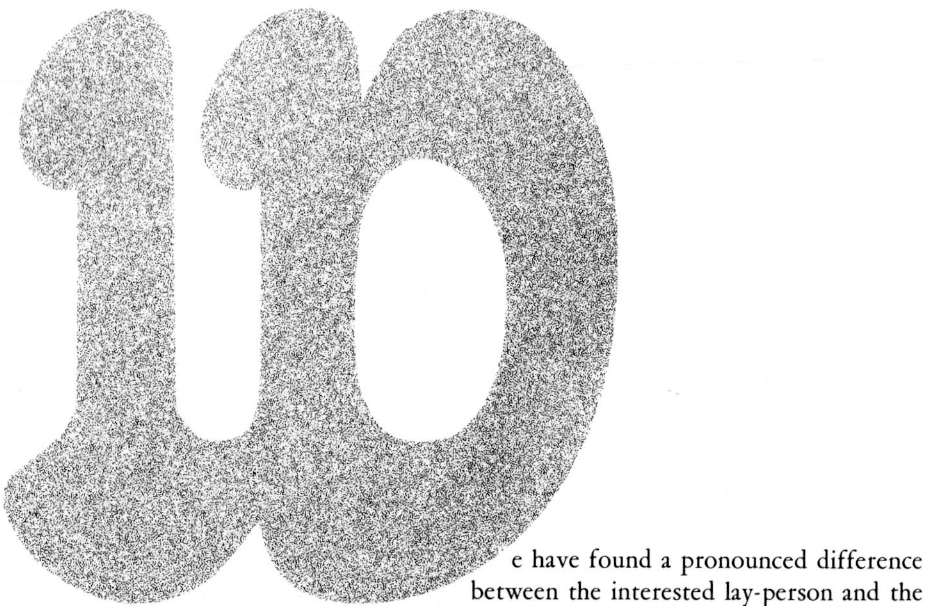

We have found a pronounced difference between the interested lay-person and the research scientist in their perception of and attitude towards the studies that have been conducted on humpback whales. The scientist tends to assess the value of the research from the viewpoint of its reliability, the sophistication and elegance of the methodology, and the theoretical value of the data analysis and interpretation. In a sense, "good" research is that which advances our knowledge, whether or not there is a short-term pay-off in terms of impact on the whale itself. The lay-person is somewhat more impatient. For the public, "good" research is that which has fairly immediate practical applications and consequences. This difference is reflected in the high frequency with which we are asked the following two questions: "Why aren't the humpback whales in the North Pacific showing clear signs of recovery if they have been protected for more than twenty years?" and "What good has all this research done the humpback whale?" There is a great deal that we have yet to learn about humpbacks, and the public wants to know why.

We cannot emphasize strongly enough that the many mysteries which remain to be solved are every bit as frustrating to us as to others with an interest in whales. Nonetheless, when one considers the practical aspects of studying free-roaming cetaceans, it is a miracle we have learned as much as we have about living whales. The

Data collected from shore stations, aerial surveys and small boat operations have helped establish the importance of non-invasive research techniques in field studies of humpback whales.

study of whale behavior is a relatively recent enterprise. It is a challenging and difficult pursuit. With few exceptions, the energy expended in data collection has outweighed the number of questions answered. One can choose to be like the optimist who sees the doughnut, or the pessimist who sees only the hole. We favor optimism tinged with a heavy dose of realism. While we now know sorrowfully little about humpbacks, what we do know far exceeds what could have been said about the biology and behavior of humpback whales a decade ago.

We feel that during the next ten years quantum leaps will continue to occur in the number of questions answered. It is instructive to consider the value of the research trends that have developed to date, and to anticipate what future developments we might expect to observe. There have been at least three highly significant applications of field study results to problems associated with humpback whales. While a few central characters played major roles in each of these examples, the successes were due to the efforts of many.

As a result of evidence collected from shore stations and aerial surveys, researchers concluded that use of the island of Kahoolawe as a military target for ship-to-shore bombardment during the whale season was keeping whales out of the area. Military officials responded by scheduling their activities at times other than during the whale season. Recent aerial surveys that we carried out indicate that

In October 1985, Humphrey the "Wayward Humpback Whale," wandered up the Sacramento River. Scientists, federal and state agencies, and the general public worked together to save the whale, finally luring it out of the river three weeks after it entered.

humpbacks are more frequently observed around Kahoolawe than was the case in earlier years.

Because of a common interest in conservation and protection of the humpback whale, commercial boat operators in Hawaii formed an association aimed at improving the operational procedures of commercial vessels in the vicinity of humpback whales. They are also interested in providing sighting data to researchers in order to help monitor temporal changes in the numbers and locations of whales across the season.

Perhaps the most dramatic demonstration of the importance of field studies of whales involved Humphrey, the "Wayward Humpback Whale," who wandered up California's Sacramento River in October of 1985. Humphrey appeared to be disoriented, and was losing fresh water that threatened his/her health and chance to find his/her way back to the ocean. After more than two weeks of failed attempts to scare Humphrey out of the river, the call went out all over North America for help. Louis Herman, at the University of Hawaii, suggested a different approach. Why not try to lure the whale out of the river? He knew of some feeding sounds that had been recorded in Alaska by his students. They had played the feeding sounds to whales in Hawaii during the breeding season, and found that the whales approached the source of the sounds. A copy of the sounds was sent to San Francisco. Other scientists took the sounds out on a boat and played them through a large underwater speaker. Upon hearing the feeding sounds, Humphrey swam to the sound playback boat, and followed the boat for more than 40 miles, until darkness set in seven hours later. The next day, the sounds were used again, and Humphrey finally made it back to the ocean, where he was last seen heading south, probably to Mexico. (Humphrey has never been photographed in Hawaiian waters.)

Only through a series of studies carried out in Alaska and Hawaii was it discovered that humpbacks made a wide variety of sounds under different circumstances. By carrying out playback studies in Hawaii, the remarkable effect of the feeding sounds was demonstrated. These research findings showed great practical use in helping to get Humphrey out of the Sacremento River.

As research continues on humpback whales in Hawaii, efforts will undoubtedly maintain a focus on the following problems:

1. DISTRIBUTION AND ABUNDANCE. Aerial, boat and shore-based observations will continue to provide more and more accurate assessments of the number of humpback whales which come to Hawaii each winter, the seasonal trends in migration in and out of the island chain, and patterns of geographical distribution. One of the major accomplishments will be the discovery of humpback whale migratory routes between the summer feeding grounds and the winter breeding grounds. This will involve the technology currently being developed through the application of short-term radio tracking devices to determine local movement patterns of humpback whales in Alaska and in the North Pacific, as well as the use of high-altitude photographic techniques perfected during studies of bowhead whale movement in the Arctic, and gray whale movement along the west coast of the United States.

2. MONITORING HABITAT QUALITY. There is a growing concern that a variety of human-induced changes in the quality of the ocean environment may threaten the recovery of endangered marine mammal stocks. Heavy metals, organochlorines (such as PCBs and DDT), and radioactive materials are being detected in worrisome quantities throughout the world's oceans. Their means of introduction into the ecosystem, their impact on ocean dwellers, and their effects on the food chain are all high priority concerns. Other threats to the humpback whale's habitat include shoreline development in Hawaii and Alaska which may introduce noise and/or pollutants; increased aerial and vessel traffic; and competition for access to highly-preferred ocean recreation areas. The effects of all of these factors will be studied in considerable detail.

3. CLARIFICATION OF THE DYNAMICS OF SOCIAL INTERACTION. Efforts will continue to document the life history of identified individual whales. Behavioral observations will provide further clarification of the utilization and functions of the behavioral displays described earlier. Acoustic techniques will be used to locate and track singers. Studies of the effects of playing back whale vocalizations will allow better interpretations of the functions of various vocalization patterns, including the song. Indisputable observations of calving and mating will provide greater insight into rates of population growth.

4. DEVELOPMENT OF A HUMPBACK WHALE RECOVERY PLAN. Perhaps the most important development which could occur during the next decade would be the successful implementation of a management and recovery plan. A recovery plan is an officially sanctioned blue-print for restoring an endangered species to a status which no longer requires protection under the Endangered Species Act (1973, as amended). The National Marine Fisheries Service (NMFS) is the governmental agency charged by Congress with responsibility for ensuring the protection and conservation of endangered marine mammals. Part of NMFS' mandate is to develop and implement such a plan in conjunction with specialists in the field, and qualified

lay-persons who may be able to provide the background data necessary for the identification of the most effective means for ensuring the humpback whale's recovery.

To date, the priorities established by NMFS have not appeared to recognize the extremely tenuous status of the humpback whale. In large part, this has been a result of a lack of clear information on such things as numbers, impact of human activity, and so on. However, a very important function to be served by a recovery team would be the designation of data gaps, recommendations regarding the most needed research activities, and the identification of those agencies or individuals most qualified to carry out the required studies. We strongly encourage NMFS to actively work toward the development of a recovery plan, and in doing so echo the recommendations made by numerous workshops convened during the past decade or so to consider the problems and future hopes for the humpback whale.

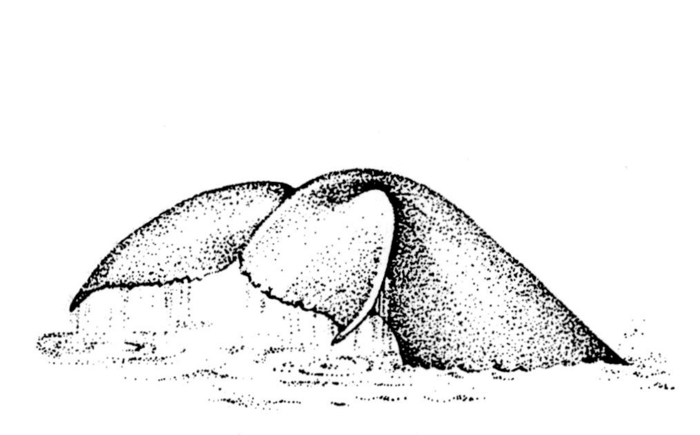

WHEREFORE, FOR ALL THESE things, we account the whale immortal in his species, however perishable in his individuality. He swam the seas before the continents broke water; he once swam over the site of the Tuileries, and Windsor Castle, and the Kremlin. In Noah's flood he despised Noah's Ark; and if ever the world is to be again flooded, like the Netherlands, to kill off its rats, then the eternal whale will still survive, and rearing upon the topmost crest of the equatorial flood, spout his frothed defiance to the skies.

from Herman Melville, *Moby Dick.*

APPENDIX A

Guide to Whales and Dolphins of Hawaii

Five species of baleen and 19 species of toothed whales are presently known to live in or migrate to waters surrounding Hawaii. Following are the scientific classifications of these species arranged under two suborders, Mysticeti (baleen) and Odontoceti (toothed) whales. For each species we provide both the common name and the latin scientific name, as well as a short description of the size and unique body characteristics. In addition, we indicate the probability of sighting each species in Hawaiian waters and/or the frequency with which they have been found stranded on the shores of the major Hawaiian Islands. Much of this information has been derived from accounts compiled by Dr. Edward Shallenberger.

CLASSIFICATION

KINGDOM:	Animalia	all animals
PHYLUM:	Chordata	possessing a notocord (a precursor to a backbone)
SUBPHYLUM:	Vertebrata	all animals with backbones
CLASS:	Mammalia	animals which suckle their young
ORDER:	Cetacea	whales, dolphins and porpoises

SUBORDER: Mysticeti — Baleen Whales

FAMILY: Balaenopteridae — Rorqual Whales

COMMON NAME: Fin Whale
SPECIES NAME: *Balaenoptera physalus*
DESCRIPTION: Second in size only to the blue whale; length averages 65 feet for males and 75 feet for females. Weight averages 60-80 tons for both sexes. Body is dark gray with right lower lip palate white. The underside of the flukes and flippers are also distinctly white. Dorsal fin is tall and the flippers relatively small, less than 15% of the body length. An average of 54 deep throat plates extend to navel.
SIGHTABILITY: Rare, there has only been one verified sighting and a single stranding.

COMMON NAME: Bryde's Whale
SPECIES NAME: *Balaenoptera edeni*
DESCRIPTION: Length averages 40 feet for males and 45 feet for females. Weight averages 20 tons for both sexes. Body is bluish-dark gray, lighter in the throat pleat area. Dorsal fin is tall and steep, and the flippers are about 10% of the body length. Easily distinguished by a series of prominent longitudinal head ridges. An average of 45 ventral grooves extend at least to the navel (photo pg. 17).
SIGHTABILITY: Rare, one photographic sighting in the last ten years.

COMMON NAME: Minke Whale
SPECIES NAME: *Balaenoptera acutorostrata*
DESCRIPTION: Length averages 25 feet for males and 30 feet for females. Weight averages 10 tons for both sexes. Body color is dark gray to black, and white on the underside of the flippers and belly. A distinct diagonal band of white is present on the dorsal portion of each flipper. The flipper is pointed and is equivalent to 12% of the body length. The dorsal fin is tall and falcate. A single prominent ridge runs longitudinally down a narrow pointed rostrum. An average of 65 throat grooves end just anterior of the navel.
SIGHTABILITY: Rare, never a sighting within the major Hawaiian island chain. However, they are sighted infrequently in the leeward islands during various times of the year.

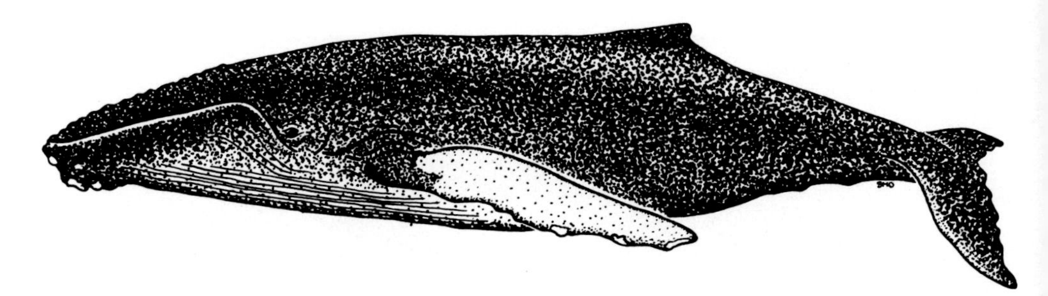

COMMON NAME: Humpback Whale
SPECIES NAME: *Megaptera novaeangliae*
DESCRIPTION: Length averages 43 feet for males and 45 feet for females. Weight averages 35 tons for both sexes. Body is black or gray dorsally, with a varying white region on the throat, flippers, belly, and the underside of the flukes. Dorsal fin ranges in size and shape, but is usually pronounced. Flippers are very long about one-third the body length, with knobs on the leading edge. Knobby protuberances are also found on the head. An average of 22 wide throat grooves extend to the navel.
SIGHTABILITY: Common inside the 100 fathom isobath from November through June.

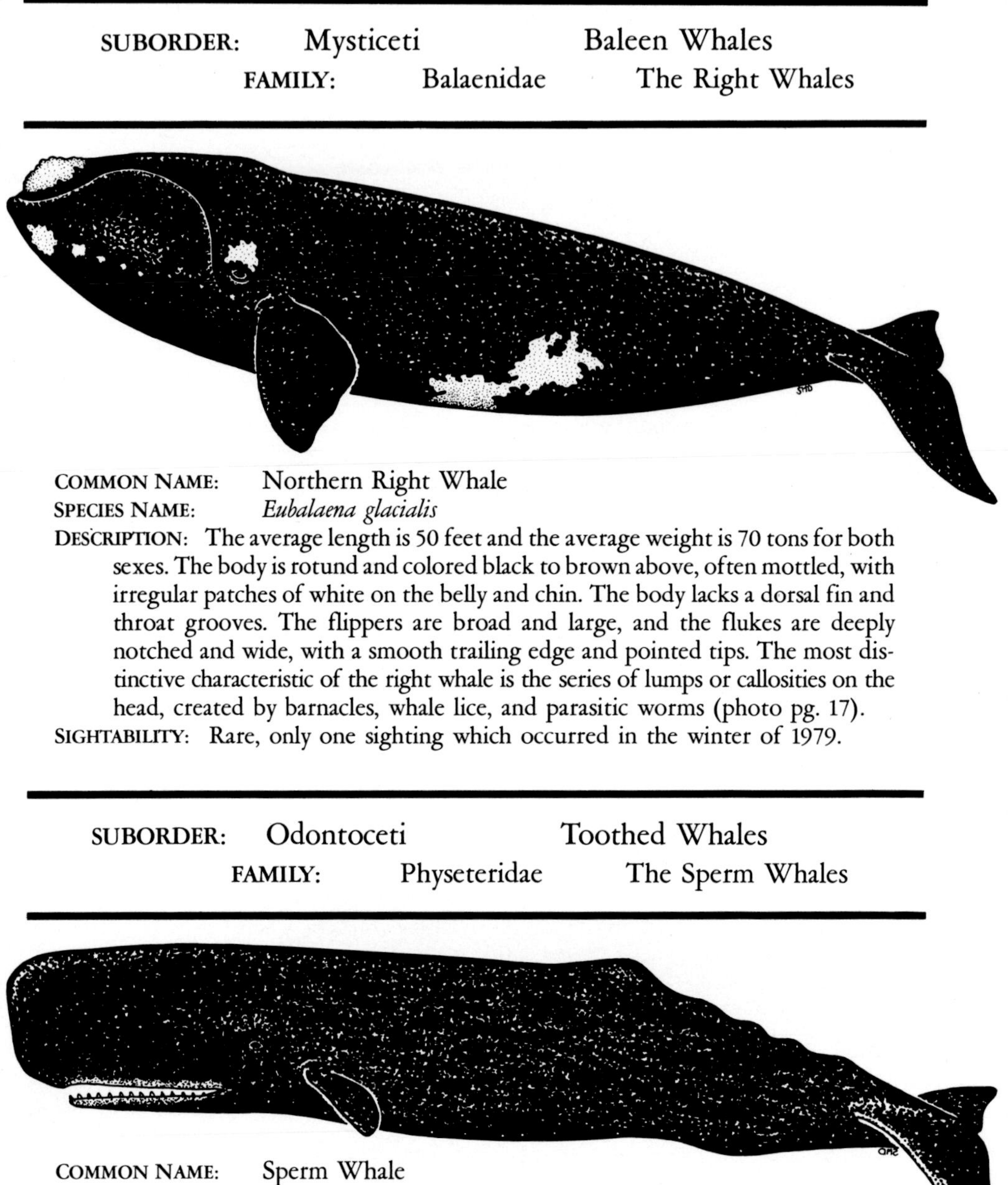

SUBORDER: Mysticeti — Baleen Whales

FAMILY: Balaenidae — The Right Whales

COMMON NAME: Northern Right Whale

SPECIES NAME: *Eubalaena glacialis*

DESCRIPTION: The average length is 50 feet and the average weight is 70 tons for both sexes. The body is rotund and colored black to brown above, often mottled, with irregular patches of white on the belly and chin. The body lacks a dorsal fin and throat grooves. The flippers are broad and large, and the flukes are deeply notched and wide, with a smooth trailing edge and pointed tips. The most distinctive characteristic of the right whale is the series of lumps or callosities on the head, created by barnacles, whale lice, and parasitic worms (photo pg. 17).

SIGHTABILITY: Rare, only one sighting which occurred in the winter of 1979.

SUBORDER: Odontoceti — Toothed Whales

FAMILY: Physeteridae — The Sperm Whales

COMMON NAME: Sperm Whale

SPECIES NAME: *Physeter macrocephalus*

DESCRIPTION: Length averages 55 feet for males and 40 feet for females, with the weights averaging 40 tons for males and 18 tons for females. The body color is dark gray to brown, with the lower jaw and belly white to off-gray. The head is large and rectangular, and the blowhole is positioned on the left side of the head. There is no true dorsal fin, instead, a dorsal hump appears two-thirds of the body length, formed by muscle and fatty tissue. There are no teeth in the upper jaw, while the lower jaw contains 18-25 pairs of conical shaped teeth. The pectoral fins are broad and stocky and the tail is wide and powerful.

SIGHTABILITY: Uncommon in the major Hawaiian island chain. Found in the springtime off the Kona coast of the Big Island. Frequently seen in the leeward island chain during the summer months (photos pg. 16, 128).

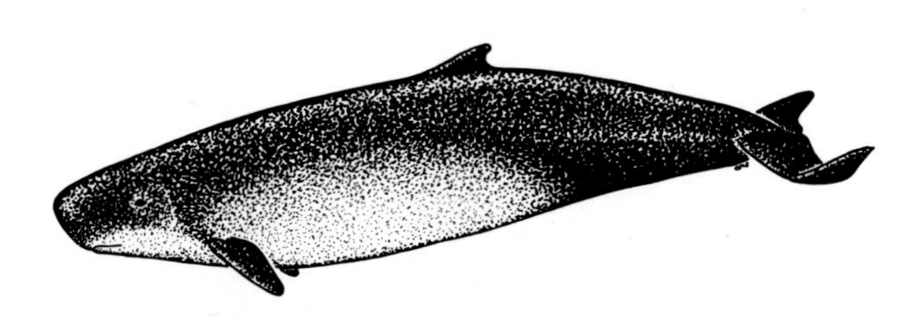

COMMON NAME: Pygmy Sperm Whale
SPECIES NAME: *Kogia breviceps*
DESCRIPTION: Size averages 10 feet and 800 pounds for both sexes. Color is dark gray above, fading to a paler gray with a distinct pink tinge below. Between the eye and flipper there is often a white or gray bracket-shaped mark; also, a pale marking is sometimes present anterior of the eye. The flippers are short and wide, and the dorsal fin is very falcate (curved) and positioned in the middle of the body. There are no functional teeth in the upper jaw, but 10 to 16 pairs of thin, curved teeth in the lower jaw.
SIGHTABILITY: Uncommon, found typically in deep offshore water with strandings occurring on the shores of the major Hawaiian Island chain.

COMMON NAME: Dwarf Sperm Whale
SPECIES NAME: *Kogia simus*
DESCRIPTION: Length averages 8 feet and weight averages 350 pounds for both sexes. Color is medium gray above, fading to a paler gray below with a pink tinge. Like the pygmy sperm whale, a near-white bracket mark or "false gill" is found between the eye and the flipper. The dorsal fin is tall and falcate. The jaw is understated with up to three pairs of rudimentary teeth in the upper jaw, and 7-12 pairs of recurved teeth in the lower jaw. Occasionally, several irregular throat grooves are present.
SIGHTABILITY: Rare, fewer than five reports of dwarf sperm whales in Hawaiian waters, all by strandings.

SUBORDER: Odontoceti — Toothed Whales

FAMILY: Delphinidae — The Oceanic Dolphins

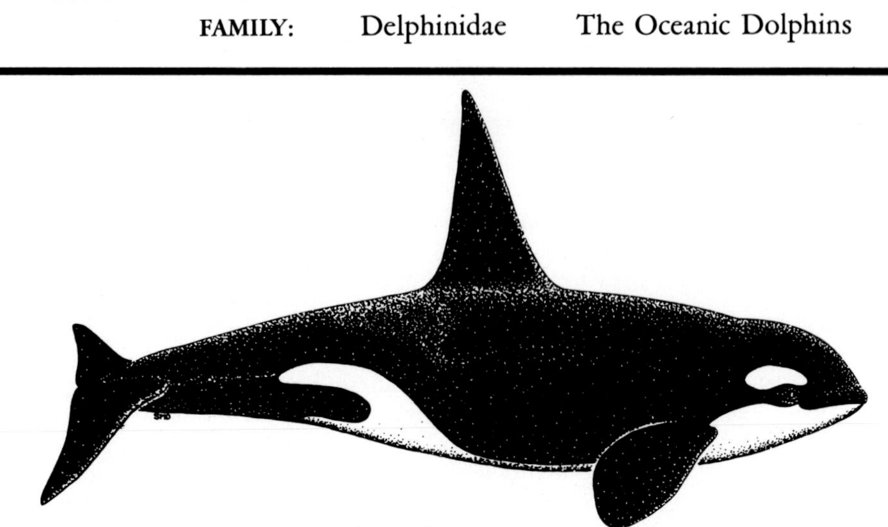

COMMON NAME: Killer Whale or Orca

SPECIES NAME: *Orcinus orca*

DESCRIPTION: Length averages 28 feet for males and 23 feet for females. The average weight is 8 tons for males and four tons for females. The body has a tall dorsal fin (especially pronounced in males), blunt round head, and large, paddle-shaped flippers. The coloration is black above, with a light gray patch, or saddle, behind the dorsal fin. The underside is white, with a conspicuous white spot above and behind the eye. There are 10-13 recurved teeth on each side of both jaws (photos pgs. 57, 62-63).

SIGHTABILITY: Rare; occasionally reported near Molokai and the Big Island, although sightings may be listed as uncommon for the leeward islands.

COMMON NAME: False Killer Whale

SPECIES NAME: *Pseudorca crassidens*

DESCRIPTION: Length averages 16 feet for males and 13 feet for females, with the weights averaging 1.25 tons for males and one ton for females. The coloration is almost all black except for a light gray area on the belly. The head is small and slender and the mouth opening is large. Pectoral fins are narrow, tapered and have a distinct broad hump on the leading edge. There are usually 8-12 large, stout teeth on each side of both jaws. Displays very little resemblance to the killer whale (photo pg. 15).

SIGHTABILITY: Common; but typically not found nearshore. Strandings of false killer whales are common in other parts of the world, but they rarely strand in Hawaii.

COMMON NAME: Pygmy Killer Whale
SPECIES NAME: *Feresa attenuata*
DESCRIPTION: Length averages 7.5 feet for males and seven feet for females; average weights are 375 and 330 pounds respectively. The coloration is dark grayish brown to black above, with sides a lighter gray and the underside white between the flippers, on the flukes, and near the genitals. The lips are also distinctively colored white. The pectoral fins are short and rounded at the tips. The head is narrow and pointed, and the dorsal fin is prominent and falcate. There are 10-13 teeth on each side of the jaws.
SIGHTABILITY: Uncommon, sightings are usually restricted to the Kona coast of the Big Island and the Waianae coast of Oahu.

COMMON NAME: Melon-headed Whale
SPECIES NAME: *Peponocephala electra*
DESCRIPTION: Length averages 7.5 feet for both sexes, with the weight averaging 350 pounds. Coloration is black above and on sides, with a pale gray patch found on the underside in the throat area. The mouthline is short and steeply angled. Pectoral fins are long and generally pointed. There are 20-25 stout teeth in each jaw.
SIGHTABILITY: Uncommon; usually found off the Big Island in water offshore. Known primarily from strandings.

COMMON NAME: Short-finned Pilot Whale
SPECIES NAME: *Globicephala macrorhynchus*
DESCRIPTION: Length averages 16 feet for males and 12 feet for females, with weights averaging 2.5 tons and 1.5 tons respectively. The coloration is primarily black or dark gray, but there is a white-to-pale gray patch on the throat, belly, and chest. A light gray patch can sometimes be found behind the eye and dorsal fin. The head is rather large and bulbous, and the dorsal fin is broadly-based and strongly curved. The pectoral fins are about 15% of the body length, and smoothly curved into a sickle shape. There are 14-18 peg-like teeth in both jaws.
SIGHTABILITY: Common; but typically not found nearshore.

COMMON NAME: Risso's Dolphin
SPECIES NAME: *Grampus griseus*
DESCRIPTION: Length averages 10 feet and weight averages 600 pounds for both sexes. The coloration is gray, fading to near-white on the face and belly, with darker gray dorsal fin, pectoral fins and tail. The body is extensively scarred from interactions with other dolphins, and the dorsal fin is tall and pointed. Pectoral fins are long and pointed. The head is squarish and distinguished by a longitudinal indentation. Normally there are no teeth in the upper jaw and no more than seven pairs of teeth in the lower jaw.
SIGHTABILITY: Rare; known only by several strandings in major island chain.

COMMON NAME: Pacific Bottlenose Dolphin
SPECIES NAME: *Tursiops gilli*
DESCRIPTION: Length averages 10 feet for males and seven feet for females; weights average 850 and 600 pounds respectively. Coloration is a mix of medium gray above with a light gray flank, fading to near white on the belly with a distinct tinge of pink. The head is robust and possesses a short stubby beak. The dorsal fin is moderately tall and falcate; pectoral fins are of medium length and pointed at the tip. There are 36 to 52 teeth in each jaw (photos pgs. 46, 47).
SIGHTABILITY: Common; can generally be observed near the major Hawaiian Islands during December through May, often swimming with humpbacks.

COMMON NAME: Rough-toothed Dolphin
SPECIES NAME: *Steno bredanensis*
DESCRIPTION: Length averages eight feet for males and seven feet for females, with respective weights for each at 300 and 250 pounds. Coloration varies from dark gray to purplish black above, with the underside being white with a light pinkish cast. There are always numerous yellow-white streaks and scars all over the body. The head gives way to a long beak giving the body a cone-shaped appearance anterior to the pectoral fins. Pectoral fins are about 15% of the total body length, and the dorsal fin is moderately tall and falcate. There are 40-54 textured teeth in each jaw.
SIGHTABILITY: Common; usually sighted in 500 fathoms or more.

COMMON NAME: Spinner Dolphin
SPECIES NAME: *Stenella longirostris*
DESCRIPTION: The length averages six feet, and weight averages 175 for both sexes. Coloration is extremely varied, making it difficult to describe a typical animal. The pattern usually consists of three colors: a dark gray on the back, a lighter gray or tan on the sides, and an even lighter gray or white on the belly. The head gives way to a long slim snout with darker gray lips and tip. The dorsal fin is usually erect and triangular, while the tail stock is usually strongly keeled in adults. Spinners average 100 teeth in each jaw.
SIGHTABILITY: Common; found throughout the Hawaiian archipelago.

COMMON NAME: Striped Dolphin
SPECIES NAME: *Stenella coeruleoalba*
DESCRIPTION: Length averages eight feet and weight average 220 pounds, with the males being slightly larger than the females. Coloration pattern varies from dark gray or bluish gray to a light gray; the sides are light gray and the belly is white. A black strip runs from the eye along the flank to the anus. This stripe may give rise to additional stripes which run to the pectoral fins and mid-way from the pectoral to the dorsal fin. The beak is always dark, and a white V-shaped blaze extends from behind the eye to the dorsal fin. The dorsal fin is slightly rounded, and the flippers are pointed. There are 90-100 slightly incurved teeth in each jaw.
SIGHTABILITY: Rare, known only from strandings.

COMMON NAME: Spotted Dolphin
SPECIES NAME: *Stenella attenuata*
DESCRIPTION: Length averages seven feet for males, 6.5 for females, with an average weight of 240 and 200 pounds respectively. Coloration is darker gray above, fading to light gray below. Spotting occurs in the adult stage, all over the body. (In Hawaii, however, the spots are fairly faint and appear to be almost absent.) The head gives way to a long, slim beak which is white tipped. The dorsal fin is tall and falcate, while the pectoral fins are of medium length and smoothly curved. There is an average of 70 teeth in each jaw.
SIGHTABILITY: Common, found throughout Hawaiian archipelago.

COMMON NAME: Common Dolphin
SPECIES NAME: *Delphinus delphis*
DESCRIPTION: The length averages 6.5 feet with weight averaging 200 pounds. Males are slightly larger than females. The coloration is black above and light gray to cream or white below. A V-shaped black or dark gray downward oriented saddle is found on the sides directly below the dorsal fin. The eyes are usually surrounded by dark circles which connect to the dark pigmentation running across the upper jaw. An hourglass effect is created on the animal's side by a unique combination of cream or yellow pigmentation. The dorsal fin is moderately pointed, and the pectoral fins are pointed. There are 80-106 pointed teeth in each jaw.
SIGHTABILITY: Rare; known only from an isolated field sighting.

COMMON NAME: Pacific White-sided Dolphin
SPECIES NAME: *Lagenoryhnchus obliquidens*
DESCRIPTION: Length averages seven feet and weight averages 200 pounds for both sexes. Coloration is a deep gray back and a white belly; the dark flanks are broken up by a variable pattern of pale gray. Above the eye and running the length of the body is a narrow white stripe which broadens in the anal area. The head gives way to a very short, thick beak. The dorsal fin is high and strongly hooked, usually dark on the leading edge. Flippers are curved with a blunted tip and are darker along the leading edge. There are 46-64 small pointed teeth in each jaw.
SIGHTABILITY: Rare; known only from an isolated field sighting.

SUBORDER: Odontoceti Toothed Whales

FAMILY: Ziphiidae

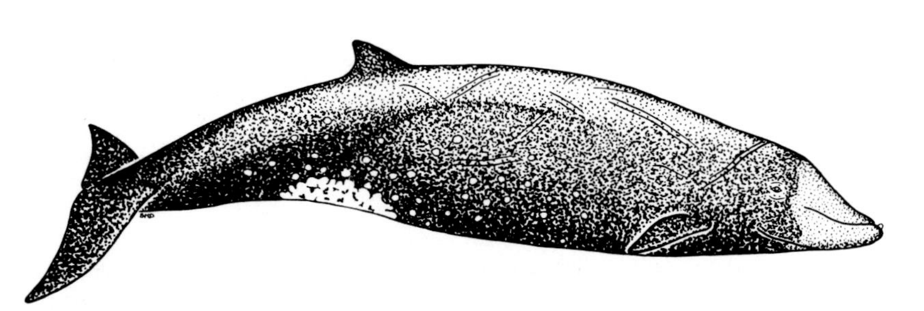

COMMON NAME: Goose Beaked or Cuvier's Beaked Whale
SPECIES NAME: *Ziphius cavirostris*

DESCRIPTION: Length averages 20 feet for males and females, average weight is four tons. Females may be slightly larger than males of the same age. Coloration varies; the back may be slate-gray or fawn colored. The small head is often lighter than the rest of the long and stocky body, which bears white or cream-colored linear and oval scars. There is a poorly defined, stubby beak; the mouth has a short cleft giving it a goose-like profile. Flippers, small and rounded, fold back into a depression on the flank. The dorsal fin is tall and has a shark-like appearance. The lower jaw juts beyond the upper, and in males contains a single pair of conical teeth at the tip.

SIGHTABILITY: Rare; known only from stranded individuals and isolated field observations.

COMMON NAME: Dense-beaked or Blainville's Beaked Whale
SPECIES NAME: *Mesoplodon densirostris*

DESCRIPTION: Length averages 15 feet and weight averages two tons in both sexes. Coloration is black or dark gray on the back, fading to slightly lighter on the abdomen, with the anal area almost white. Grayish white or pink blotching is typical, and scratches and scars usually cover the body. Flippers are short and the pointed dorsal fin is large and curved backward. The mouth has a high arching contour sweeping up over the eye, impairing forward vision. This prominence is created by a massive pair of teeth in the lower jaw. Each tooth is almost eight inches long in the males. Teeth of females are small and totally buried in the gum, but the lower jaw still has a marked bulge.

SIGHTABILITY: Rare; known only by two strandings in the Leeward islands.

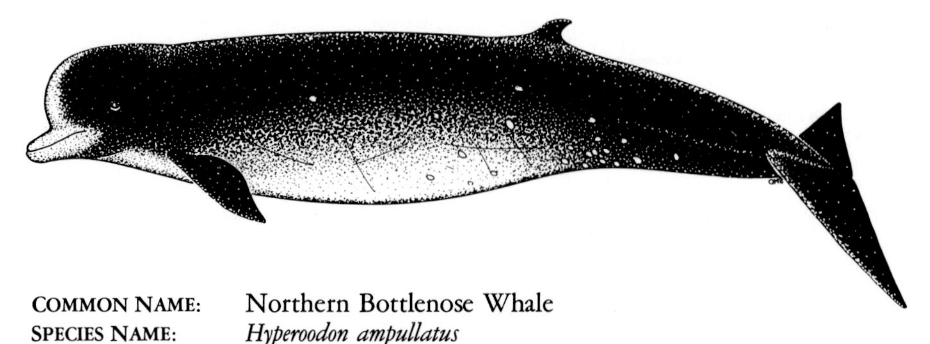

COMMON NAME: Northern Bottlenose Whale
SPECIES NAME: *Hyperoodon ampullatus*
DESCRIPTION: Length 28 feet for males and 24 feet for females, with average weights of four and three tons respectively. Coloration varies a great deal, but the back is normally a dark gray, grading to smoke gray on the belly. There is often a pale bracket or gill mark across the back of the neck area. The forehead is bulbous and pronounced. The dorsal fin is tall and hooked; flippers are short and tapered. A V-shaped pair of short grooves are found on the throat, with the open end of the V facing the tail. A pair of fully developed conical teeth, 1.5 to two inches long, are found on the tip of the lower jaw of older adult males. Females possess teeth, but they are embedded deeply in the gum, and do not erupt.
SIGHTABILITY: Rare, single isolated sighting varified by photographs.

APPENDIX B

Whalewatching Tips

Watching whales can be a rewarding and exciting activity. It requires little equipment, only a small amount of practice, but a great deal of patience. Whales can be observed from land, sea, or air depending on their proximity to shore and the time and money one is willing to spend searching for them. Since all cetaceans found in U.S. waters are protected by the Marine Mammal Protection Act, one should make inquiries about special rules or regulations which may apply to the species of interest (see page 157).

Humpback whales may be observed in Hawaii from November through May, although they have been reported as early as October and as late as July. The likelihood of seeing a whale decreases with increases in sea states, wind speed, sun glare, or other conditions which may hamper visibility. In Hawaii this can include smoke and ashes from burning sugar cane. Midday is the preferred time to observe whales from land or air, since the sun is near-directly overhead. Watching whales from a boat is more dependent upon weather and less influenced by time of day.

EQUIPMENT

Whalewatching allows you the opportunity to either use very little equipment or depending upon your desire, to equip yourself with a veritable gaggle of gadgets. During our years of whale research, we have tried and tested almost every new "mousetrap" that has been touted as "required equipment for the complete whalewatcher." In the following section we recommend what we have found to be the most useful and efficient pieces of optional equipment.

BINOCULARS can help to bring you closer to the whales and provide more detailed observation of their behaviors. Binoculars come in a variety of sizes, weights, colors, and magnifications. When viewing whales from land we suggest 10x50 wide angle binoculars. These will bring the whales ten times closer than the unaided eye. While this magnification is helpful from land, it can be difficult to hold these binoculars steady if you plan on watching whales from a boat or airplane. If your whalewatching plans include field trips on the water or in the air, consider a pair of 8x40 or 7x50 wide angle binoculars instead.

Rubber coated binoculars are a bit more expensive, but seem to withstand abuse from close encounters with boat decks, rocks, doors, and other whalewatchers. Most rubberized binoculars are not waterproof. Waterproof binoculars cost four to five times more than normal binoculars. We prefer binoculars with individual focus mechanisms that can be accurately adjusted for our own eyes. Center-focus binoculars get a bit sloppy as they age, causing undue eyestrain.

When purchasing binoculars, try them out first, and learn how to use them properly. During encounters with thousands of whalewatchers we have found that many do not know how to operate or care for their binoculars. To tell if a pair of prospective binoculars are right for you, focus the binoculars on an object about 100 yards away. If at the end of one minute, your eyes feel unstrained and you can hold the binoculars comfortably steady, they are probably right for you. Remember that you can impair your vision with improperly adjusted or poorly maintained binoculars.

Scan the horizon for at least 30 minutes to determine if whales are in the area. Make certain to hold your camera steady and slowly depress your shutter to assure a good photograph.

Take care never to look into direct or bright sunlight with your binoculars!

TELESCOPES: Some whalewatchers prefer using telescopes for watching whales from land. Telescopes can bring you closer to the whales, but they can be frustrating to operate. A telescope's field of vision is typically very narrow and the whale will be constantly moving out of your view. In addition to increased magnification, a telescope requires less energy to operate than binoculars because it is supported by a tripod. A tripod can be fitted, however, to your binoculars to give the ease of telescope operation coupled with the comfortable stereo-field of the binoculars.

PHOTOGRAPHIC TIPS: We have never met a whalewatcher who hasn't dreamed of taking the ultimate whale photograph. Capturing exciting images of whales on film takes a lot of time, a touch of intuition, and a good deal of luck. You should probably first consider if you really want to take photographs during your whalewatch. That may sound peculiar, but it is important to realize that a camera can actually get in the way of your whalewatching experience. When a whale breaches close to the boat, it may be more rewarding to just watch it roll in mid-air and crash back onto the water rather than fumbling with your camera in a vain attempt to remember all the procedures necessary for the camera's operation.

Good photographs of whales can be taken with any type of camera, but for ease of operation and flexibility we recommend a 35 mm single lense reflex (SLR). These allow you to use a variety of lenses which are readily available and easily changed. We prefer to use a 300mm lens from boats and planes, and a 600 mm lens for land based observations. Remember that too many lenses can become costly and bulky, and usually one does not have the time to change lenses when necessary. An 80–200 mm zoom is probably the best general purpose lens to purchase. It gives you wide flexibility in whalewatching as well as other photographic activities.

The photographs in this book were obtained using 35 mm cameras and primarily 64 ASA Kodachrome transparency film (black and white images were derived from the color transparencies). We prefer using slide film because it gives a slightly thicker negative to work with and allows for more flexibility in its use. Light is seldom a problem in Hawaii, so use a color print or slide film with an ASA/ISO of 50 to 100. Use a color print or slide film of 400 ASA/ ISO when whalewatching from the air in order to minimize the effect of aircraft vibration. Always bring plenty of film with you, it never fails that you will have the best whalewatching experience the day you have only brought along one spare roll! To get fine photographs of whales you have to practice, which means taking a lot of bad pictures of whales before you develop your own technique. We took about 1,000 pictures for every good photograph we published in this book!

Taking photographs of whales takes a great deal of patience and intuition. You are bound to get a lot of pictures of splashes before you capture a breaching whale in mid-air!

BASIC RULES: Whether you use an instamatic camera or one with a sophisticated large format, there are several basic rules to follow when attempting to photograph whales. Hold your camera steady. Make certain that the horizon line is level in your viewfinder. Slowly depress the shutter release. Never follow the whale through its movements while taking a picture as this will blur the image. Set your shutter speed for at least 500th of a second; this will freeze the movement of the whale, the vessel (or aircraft), the ocean, and your body. When using a camera equipped with a light meter, set the correct aperture by aiming your camera on the water in the direction of the whale, not on the sky and water. Since the whale is emerging from the water and not from the sky, this will give the proper color balance for the whale and the water, with the sky being slightly over-exposed.

FILTERS will enhance your photographs. A UV or skylight filter can reduce the brightness of the sky and the water's glare with a minimal effect on shutter speed or aperture setting. A polarizing filter will greatly reduce glare and increase water penetration of your photographs. This will however, result in the loss of one to two f-stops. A tripod is not useful for water and aerial work, but is recommended for photographs from shore.

VIDEO OR MOVIE: If using video or movie cameras to film whales, the same general rules for taking still photographs apply. Avoid excessive zooming in and out on the whales, as this will only serve to greatly accentuate the motion of the vessel or aircraft. Also, it is very important to know that you can severly damage a video camera (and your eyes) by filming directly into bright, glaring sunlight.

Sometimes whales may venture closely to a whalewatching boat. Be prepared for the possibility of your camera equipment becoming wet from the blow or splash of a curious whale.

CLOTHING/SUNSCREEN: Always take precautions to protect your skin from the sun. Use a sun cream that has a protection factor of 15 (allowing you to stay out in the sun 15 times longer than unprotected skin), and will not wear off when you become wet. A visor or hat and sunglasses will make viewing more pleasant. Wear loose fitting, light-colored cotton clothing. Be prepared for the possibility of getting wet from water over the bow of the boat, the blow of a nearby whale or rain. A water-proof case for your equipment is recommended; we have improvised many times with large plastic garbage bags. Remember "Salt Kills:" one drop of salt water in the working parts will destroy most cameras and electronic equipment.

SEASICKNESS: Even the most seasoned whalewatcher or sailor can become seasick. We recall a memorable whalewatch when the ocean was flat calm and the whales were performing superbly. Everyone on board was having a grand time except one elderly woman. Her husband, an experienced sailor, was comforting her while extolling the virtues of being a good sailor. Shortly, however, she began to "feed the fishes," and — lo and behold his stomach weakened too. Not only did he loose his pride overboard but his dentures as well!

Becoming seasick can definitely cast a pallor over your whalewatching experience. If you have ever experienced motion sickness or discomfort previously, we would suggest that you take some prophylactic measures beforehand. Unfortunately most whalewatchers wait until it is too late before seeking medicinal relief. Take your medication before the trip, at least a half hour in advance. Some medications can cause drowsiness; we have found that food containing ginger, such as ginger cookies and ginger ale, is helpful.

It helps to be well rested and relaxed before your trip. Have a light meal an hour or two beforehand and avoid eating greasy food while onboard. Crackers or dry bread and fruit (especially papaya) are good snack items. If you become thirsty, sip on carbonated beverages; avoid alcohol. Stand near the center of the vessel and keep your eyes trained on the horizon. The bow (front) of the vessel will have the roughest ride; the stern (rear) will provide a smoother ride but less desired than the center of the vessel because of exhaust fumes from the engines. Stay out in the open air but avoid too much sunshine. Do not go below decks and refrain (if possible) from going to the bathroom (nautical head), since it is usually small and claustrophobic. Talk to your fellow whalewatchers to help take your mind off your queasy state.

If all else fails, walk to the rear of the vessel, casually lean overboard, act like you are looking for tropical fish, and "heave to."

WHALEWATCHING FROM SHORE

When observing whales from the shore it is best to chose an elevated area with a wide, unobstructed view. With the naked eye, scan the horizon back and forth for at least 30 minutes. The most obvious visual clues to a whale's presence are a blow or splashing caused by surface activity. The whale's blow will appear like a puff of smoke at the water's surface, ascend 10 - 20 feet above the water and linger for up to one minute depending upon the wind. On windy days, novice whalewatchers often mistake whitecaps and minor water spouts for whales. A good rule of thumb to remember: the blow of a humpback is a lingering event when compared to the quick, sporadic splashes caused by weather and sea conditions.

During the winter months, humpback whales can be viewed from the shorelines on every major Hawaiian island. The following are a few preferred locations at which the likelihood of seeing whales is quite high.

Selected Whalewatching Sites Throughout The Hawaiian Islands.

Niihau and Kahoolawe are closed to the general public.

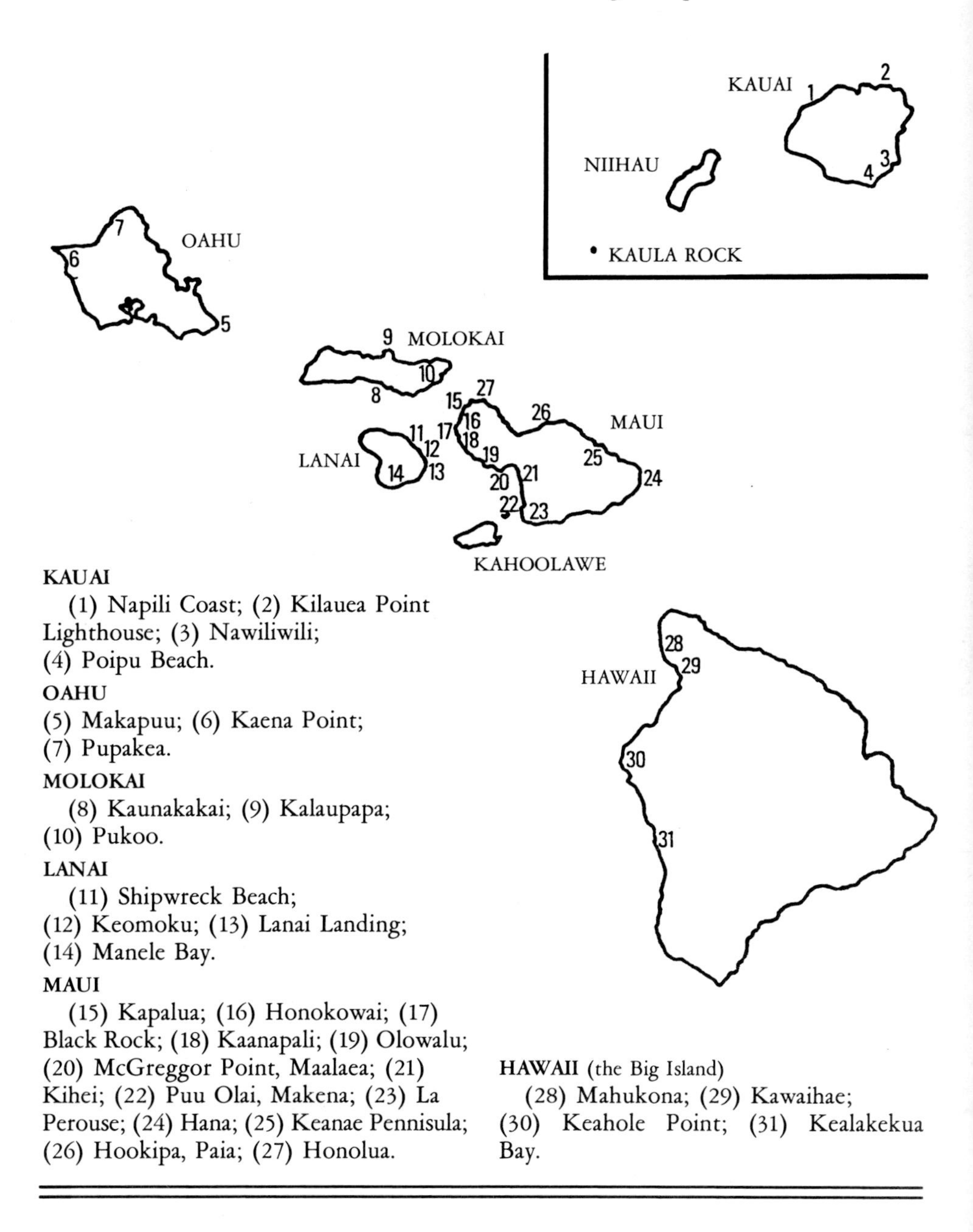

KAUAI

(1) Napili Coast; (2) Kilauea Point Lighthouse; (3) Nawiliwili; (4) Poipu Beach.

OAHU

(5) Makapuu; (6) Kaena Point; (7) Pupakea.

MOLOKAI

(8) Kaunakakai; (9) Kalaupapa; (10) Pukoo.

LANAI

(11) Shipwreck Beach; (12) Keomoku; (13) Lanai Landing; (14) Manele Bay.

MAUI

(15) Kapalua; (16) Honokowai; (17) Black Rock; (18) Kaanapali; (19) Olowalu; (20) McGreggor Point, Maalaea; (21) Kihei; (22) Puu Olai, Makena; (23) La Perouse; (24) Hana; (25) Keanae Pennisula; (26) Hookipa, Paia; (27) Honolua.

HAWAII (the Big Island)

(28) Mahukona; (29) Kawaihae; (30) Keahole Point; (31) Kealakekua Bay.

An aerial view of a humpback whale performing a peduncle slap.

WHALEWATCHING FROM THE AIR

Spotting whales from an airplane can be quite difficult and takes a fair amount of practice. Small, light, high-winged, propeller driven aircraft work best. The optimum flying height is 1000 feet with an air speed of 100 mph. When an animal is sighted, it may be necessary to circle or 'orbit' above it to increase viewing. All in all, whalewatching from aircraft is rather limited—only brief encounters with whales are possible since the aircraft cannot stop in one spot and observe the animals for an extended period.

Helicopters are poor aircraft to watch whales from because they appear to evoke fright reactions from humpbacks.

WHALEWATCHING FROM BOATS

To spot a whale from the water, merely scan the horizon, looking for a blow or surface activity. In a large body of water with no visible landmarks, it can be difficult to point out to others the actual location of a pod. To keep a keen track of the pod, think of your boat as a large clock with the bow at 12 o'clock and the stern at 6 o'clock. When a pod surfaces, it can easily be located and tracked by the 'time' in which it appears on your large floating clock.

The best method for approaching whales is to parallel the animals slowly and slightly to the rear, at a distance no less than 100 yards (or the posted minimum approach limit, see opposite page). Avoid sudden engine speed or vessel direction changes. Always give pods accompanied by calves a wide berth, and never inhale the blow of any cetacean—they can carry many air-borne diseases.

HYDROPHONES: Many cetacean sounds can be heard through the hull of the boat if the animals are nearby. Have the captain shut-down the vessel's engines and place your ear against the side of the boat. The humpback's song will sound like a "barnyard chorus," while dolphins will emit high frequency whistles and chirps.

Some boats are equipped with hydrophones (underwater microphones) in order to hear the sounds created by cetaceans. It is not necessary to go through the expense of buying a hydrophone (prices range from $200 upwards) to hear and record cetacean sounds. A decent recording system can be devised by connecting a small cassette tape recorder to an external microphone that is wrapped in several small plastic bags sealed tightly shut with good adhesive tape. To begin recording, stop the boat's engine and lower your new hydrophone (on the whale side of the boat) into the water about eight feet (to help reduce surface and vessel noise). Turn the cassette recorder on. Hold the hydrophone cable away from the boat to keep it from hitting and ruining your recording. It is a good idea to never let go of your hydrophone; a number of whale researchers have made this costly error, automatically becoming life members of P. H. Forestell's Lost Hydrophone Club.

APPENDIX C

Whalewatching Regulations

To provide more effective protection for humpback whales in Hawaii, the National Marine Fisheries Service has published a list of activities which will be presumed to constitute harassment of these animals—and therefore violations of the law under the Endangered Species Act of 1973 (as amended) and the Marine Mammal Protection Act of 1972 (as amended).

In all areas within 200 nautical miles of the islands of Hawaii the following activities are considered violations:

A) VESSELS, SWIMMERS and DIVERS

Approaching within 100 yards of a humpback whale; herding or driving a humpback whale from any distance; multiple changes in vessel speed; traveling faster than a whale (or the slowest whale in a group); or separating a cow from a calf. In addition, activities are restricted to 300 yards within all inshore waters from Hekili Point at Olowalu to Puu Olai at Makena, Maui; and within two miles of the northeast coast of Lanai.

B) AIRCRAFT

Flying lower than 1000 feet while within a horizontal distance of 300 yards from a whale. This includes hovering over, circling around, or buzzing whales.

C) GENERAL

Any other act of omission which substantially disrupts the normal behavior of a whale is also presumed to constitute harassment. A substantial disruption of normal behavior may be manifested by, among other actions on the part of the whales, a rapid change in direction or speed; escape tactics such as prolonged diving, underwater course changes, underwater exhalation, or evasive swimming patterns; interruption of breeding or nursing activities; attempts by a whale to shield a calf from a vessel or human observer by tail swishing or by other protective movements; or the abandonment of a previously frequented area.

Cooperation in adhering to these restrictions is essential for the protection of these endangered animals. *These restrictions are, incidentally, subject to change from time to time.* For further information, or harassment complaints, contact: Western Pacific Program Office, National Marine Fisheries Service, P.O. Box 3830, Honolulu, Hawaii 96818. Phone on Oahu (808) 546-5670.

APPENDIX D

How You Can Help

The Pacific Whale Foundation (a non-profit research and conservation organization) conducts and coordinates ongoing research throughout the Pacific. In addition the Foundation hosts whale-watching cruises in Hawaii and has access to information concerning marine mammal research and whalewatching throughout the world.

Donations and requests for information should be addressed to: PACIFIC WHALE FOUNDATION, P.O. Box 1038, Kihei, HI 96753. Or call (808) 879-8811.

A mass stranding of over 100 pilot whales off Great Barrier Island, New Zealand. Scientists and volunteers worked endlessly to keep the whales cool and wet, and shaded from direct sunlight. In the end, 67 of the animals were saved.

Aiding stranded whales can be both frustrating and dangerous. Turning your back on a flailing animal could result in serious injuries.

APPENDIX E
Strandings

Each year hundreds of whales, dolphins, and porpoises are found washed up on beaches. The exact cause of most strandings is often unknown, giving rise to a variety of speculative theories.

Humpback and other baleen whales rarely strand; and when they do, it almost invariably involves a single animal. Toothed whales often mass strand. This has given support to one stranding theory which suggests that the advanced echolocation capabilities of the toothed whales become impaired, causing them to strand.

Recent studies reveal that greater than 80 percent of all strandings have occurred in areas of low magnetic fields, caused by electrical storms. Many migratory animals possess a metaloid substance called magnetite. Magnetite has been detected in the brains of humpback whales, bottlenose dolphins, birds and fish. It is thought that these animals utilize magnetite to detect the polarity of the earth, and thereby orient themselves when traveling great distances. The magnetic disturbances caused by electrical storms may be sufficient to disorient whales and cause them to strand.

Humpback whales are susceptible to various ailments, including hypertension, cirrhosis of the liver, pneumonia, stomach ulcers, meningitis and syphylis, plus any of a number of airborne diseases which may be transmitted through the blow. It is important not to forget the hazards of contracting a communicable disease when rushing to the aid of a beached whale. Take necessary precautions at all times.

Since whales are ocean dwelling mammals, there is no logical reason why they would want to come to land to die. (A sick or weak whale can, of course, be caught by the incoming tide and washed ashore.) Whatever the reason a whale strands, once its body loses the buoyant support of seawater, gravity begins to take its toll. Internal organs can be damaged, and respiration can become difficult when the animal cannot maintain its upright horizontal breathing position. The same high-volume to low-surface-area adaptation which helps the whale retain its heat in the water, quickly works against the animal on land as it cannot disperse heat quickly enough and begins to "cook" internally.

Aiding stranded whales can be a very frustrating and tiring experience. In 90 percent of the strandings the animals die, and quite often we never learn why. The following is a suggested format on how to deal with stranded whales.

HELPING STRANDED WHALES

1. When you see a stranded whale, immediately call the National Marine Fisheries Service or your State Fish and Wildlife agent (in Hawaii you need only dial 911). All whales, whether dead or alive, are protected by the Marine Mammal Protection Act.

2. When officials arrive, take their advice. Only assist if requested to do so. Your biggest contribution at this point could be helping control sightseers.

3. Keep sightseers back—excessive noise and people may further stress the animal. Helicopters and low flying aircraft can also cause stress.

IF FEDERAL OR STATE AGENTS are unavailable or delayed, initiate the following:

4. If the animal is alive, make sure that the blowhole is clear, and respiration is possible.

5. Keep the animal's skin wet, taking care not to pour water down its blowhole. If the animal is out of water, ice packs may be sparingly applied to the fins and fluke to cool circulating blood.

6. If the animal is on its side, try and dig a hollow area in the sand so it can be righted on its stomach. Always take caution never to inhale the blow. Stay clear of the tail—you may easily be injured by flailing.

7. Try and shade the animal from direct sunlight. Apply zinc cream, lanolin, or other sunblocking agents to the upper portion of the animal. Never use suntan oils or lotions!

8. If possible, try and refloat the whale(s), keeping the blowhole(s) above the water. A gentle rocking motion may help it to recover the equilibrium it lost in the stranding. Take caution to handle the animal as little as possible since it might carry infectious diseases.

9. In the case of mass stranding, concentrate your aid on the animals still in the water. Keep them upright, and never pull or push the head, flippers or tails.

10. Above all remain calm, and be aware of your safety as well as of those around you. If you were unable to contact the proper officials and the animal dies or is dead, make sure you contact the local Public Health Office for disposal of the carcass.

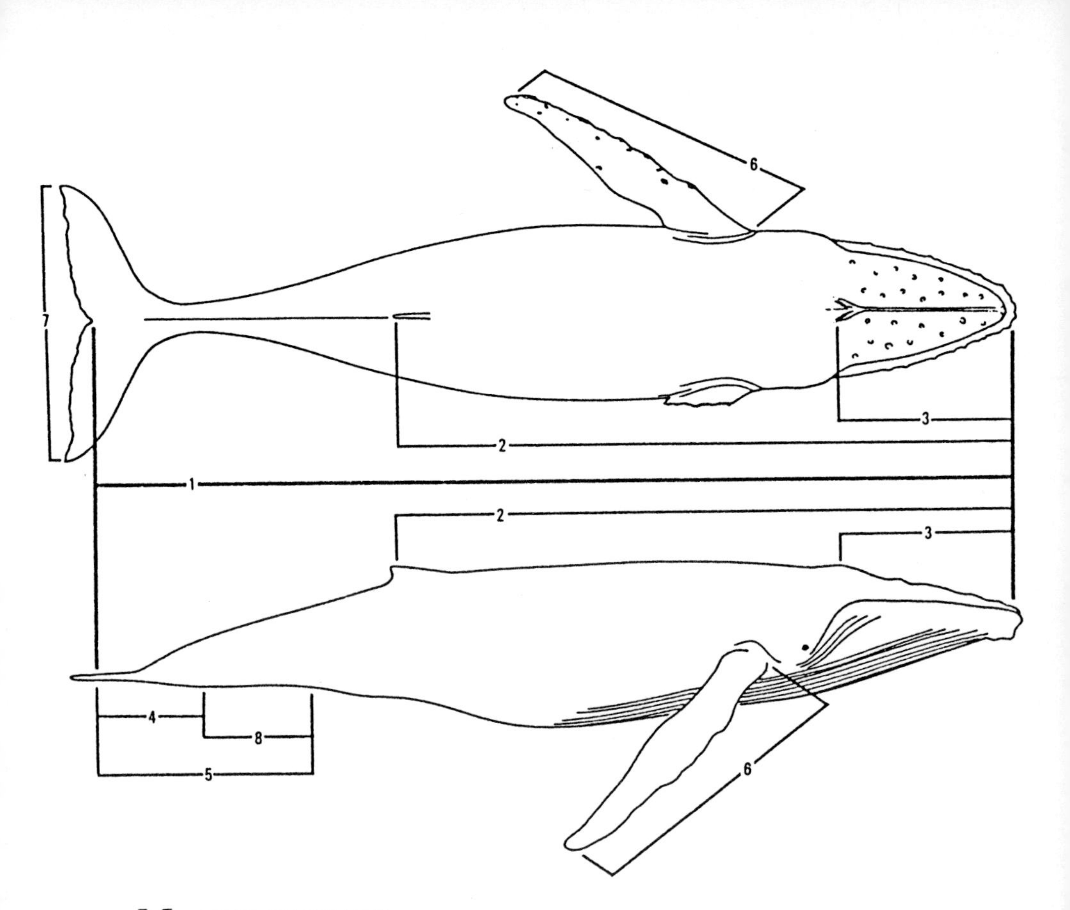

MEASUREMENTS

Important facts can be gleaned from stranded whales. If a camera is available take photographs of the entire animal, plus close-ups of the head, dorsal fin, fluke (dorsal and ventral if possible), flippers and genital region.

Basic measurements can be recorded from a stranded whale if a tape measure is handy; make certain to take them in straight lines and not over the curves of the body. The following measurements should be made and reported:

1. Total body length—tip of snout to deepest part of notch between tail flukes.
2. Tip of snout to the highest point of dorsal fin.
3. Length of snout to blowholes.
4. Anus to deepest part of notch between tail flukes.
5. Genital aperture to deepest part of notch between tail flukes.
6. Flipper length.
7. Width of tail flukes (tip to tip).
8. Distance between genital aperture and anus.

INFORMATION should be sent to: Marine Mammal Events Program, Smithsonian Institute National Museum of Natural History, Washington, D.C. 20560.

Selected Bibliography

THIS LIST OF SOURCES is prepared for the benefit of readers interested in learning more about whales, especially the humpback, and does not attempt to include all the works consulted in the preparation of this book.

GENERAL

Allen, K. Radway. 1980. *Conservation and Management of Whales.* Washington Sea Grant Publication.

Aristotle, 355 BC. 1964. *Historia Animalium.* London: Heineman, Loeb Classical Library.

Baker, A.N. 1984. *Whales and Dolphins of New Zealand and Australia: an Identification Guide.* Wellington: Victoria University Press.

Brower, K., and W.R. Curtsinger. 1979. *Wake of the Whale.* Hutchinson/Friends of the Earth.

Bruyns, Morzer. 1971. *Field Guide to Whales and Dolphins.* Amsterdam, Netherlands: Uitgevery tor/n. v. Utgerery V.H.C.A. mess Zeiseniskade 14 II.

Bryden, M.M. and R.J. Harrison (eds.) 1985. *Research on Dolphins.* London: Oxford University Press.

Cousteau, Jacques-Yves, and Phillipe Diole. 1972. *The Whale: Mighty Monarch of the Sea.* New York: Doubleday.

Coffey, D.J. 1977. *Dolphins, Whales and Porpoises: An Encyclopedia of Marine Mammals.* New York: Collier Books.

Dawson, Stephen. 1985. *The New Zealand Whale and Dolphin Digest.* Auckland: Brick Row Publishing.

Ellis, Richard. 1981. *The Book of Whales.* New York: Alfred A. Knopf.

________. 1982. *Dolphins and Porpoises.* New York: Alfred A. Knopf.

Friends of the Earth. 1978. *The Whale Manual.* San Francisco, California: Friends of the Earth.

Frost, Hon. Sir Sydney. 1978. *Whales and Whaling.* Report of the independent inquiry conducted by the Hon. Sir Sydney Frost, Vol. 1, Vol 2. Canberra: Australian Government Publishing Service.

Gaskin, D.E. 1972. *Whales, Dolphins and Seals.* Auckland: Heinemann

________. 1982. *The Ecology of Whales and Dolphins.* London: Heinemann

Haley, D., (ed.) 1978. *Marine Mammals of Eastern North Pacific and Arctic Waters.* Seattle: Pacific Search Press.

Harrison, R.J. *Functional Anatomy of Marine Mammals.* Vols. 1 (1972), 2 (1974), and 3 (1977). London and New York: Academy Press.

________, and S.H. Ridgway. 1976. *Deep Diving in Mammals.* Durham, England: Meadowfield Press.

Herman, L.M., (ed.) 1980. *Cetacean Behavior: Mechanisms and Functions.* John Wiley and Sons, New York.

Katona, Steven; David Richardson; and Robin Hazard. 1977. *A Field Guide to the Whales and Seals of the Gulf of Maine.* 2d ed. Bar Harbor, Maine: College of the Atlantic.

Kraus, S., and S. Katona, (eds.) 1977. Humpback whales *(Megaptera novaeangliae)* in the Western North Atlantic - a catalogue of identified individuals. Bar Harbor, ME: College of the Atlantic.

Leatherwood, S.; R. Reeves; W.F. Perrin; and W.E. Evans. 1982. *Whales, Dolphins and Porpoises of the Eastern North Pacific and Adjacent Arctic Waters: A Guide to their Identification.* NOAA Technical Report NMFS Circular 444.

________; R. Reeves; and L. Foster. 1983. *The Sierra Club Handbook of Whales and Dolphins.* San Francisco, California: Sierra Club Books.

Lilly, J.C. 1967. *The Mind of the Dolphin.* New York: Doubleday.

Lockley, R.M. 1979. *Whales, Dolphins and Porpoises.* London: David and Charles.

McIntyre, J., (ed.) 1974. *Mind in the Waters.* New York: Charles Scribner's Sons, and San Francisco: Sierra Club Books.

Minasian, S.M.; K.C. Balcomb III; and L. Foster. 1984. *The World's Whales, The Complete Illustrated Guide.* New York: W.W. Norton & Co., Smithsonian Books.

Norris, K.S., (ed.) 1966. *Whales, Dolphins and Porpoises.* Berkeley: University of California Press.

________. 1976. *The Porpoise Watcher.* London: John Murray.

________, and R.R. Reeves (eds.) 1978. Report on a workshop on problems related to humpback whales (Megaptera novaeangliae) in Hawaii. NTIS, PB-280, Report No. MMC-77/03.

Payne, R., (ed.) 1983 *Communication and Behavior of Whales.* Boulder, CO.: Westview Press.

Pryor, K.W. 1975. *Lads Before the Wind: Adventures in Porpoise Training.* New York: Harper Row.

Purves, P.E., and G.E. Pilleri, 1983. *Echolocation in Whales and Dolphins.* New York: Academic Press Inc.

Ridgway, S.H., (ed.) 1972. *Mammals of the Sea—Biology and Medicine.* Springfield, Illinois: Thomas.

________, and R. Harrison (eds.) 1985. *Handbook of Marine Mammals,* Vol. 3, The Sirenians and Baleen Whales. New York: Academic Press.

Robson, F.D. 1976. *Thinking Dolphins, Talking Whales.* Wellington: Reed.

________. 1984. *Strandings: Ways to Save Whales.* Johannesburg: Science Press.

Scheffer, Victor B. 1969. *The Year of the Whale.* New York: Scribner.

________. 1976. *A Natural History of Marine Mammals.* New York: Scribner.

Schevill, W.E., (ed.) 1974. *The Whale Problem - A Status Report.* Cambridge, Massachusetts: Harvard University Press.

Tavolga, W.M., (ed.) 1964. *Marine Bioacoustics.* Oxford: Pergamon.

Tomilin, A.G. 1967. *Mammals of the U.S.S.R. and Adjacent Countries.* Vol. 9. Cetacea. Jerusalem: Israel Program for Scientific Translations.

Watson, Lyall. 1981. *Sea Guide to Whales of the World.* New York: Elsevier-Dutton.

Winn, H.E., and B.L. Olla., (eds.) 1979. *Behaviour of Marine Mammals—Current Perspectives in Research.* Vol. 3. New York: Plenum Press.

Winn, L.K., and H.E. Winn. 1985. *Wings in the Sea, The Humpback Whale.* Hanover: University Press of New England.

TECHNICAL

Baker, C.S., and L.M. Herman. 1981. Migration and local movement of humpback whales through Hawaiian waters. *Can. J. Zoo.,* 59: 460-469.

________, and ________. 1984a. Aggressive behavior between humpback whales, *Megaptera novaeangliae,* wintering in Hawaiian waters. *Can. J. Zoo.,* 62: 1922-1937.

________, and ________. 1984b. Seasonal contrasts in the social behavior of humpback whales. *Cetus* 5: 14-16.

________, ________, B.G. Bays, and G.B. Bauer. 1983. The impact of vessel traffic on the behavior of humpback whales in Southeast Alaska: 1982 season. Report to the National Marine Mammal Laboratory, Seattle. WA.

________, ________, ________, and W. S. Stifel. 1982. The impact of vessel traffic on the behavior of humpback whales in Southeast Alaska: 1981 season. Report to the National Marine Mammal Laboratory, Seattle, WA.

________, ________, and A. Perry. 1985. (Abstract) Geographic variation and possible sexual dimorphism in the fluke coloration of humpback whales. Vancouver, B.C.: Sixth Biennial Conference on the Biology of Marine Mammals, Nov. 22-26.

________, ________, ________, W.S. Lawton, J.M. Straley, and J.H. Straley. 1985. Population characteristics and migration of summer and late-season humpback whales *(Megaptera novaeangliae)* in southeastern Alaska. *Mar. Mam, Sci.,* 1: 304-323.

________, ________, ________, ________, A. Wolman, H. Winn, J. Hall G. Kaufman, J. Reinke, and J. Ostman. 1986. The migratory movement and population structure of humpback whales *(Megaptera novaeangliae)* in the Central and Eastern North Pacific. *Mar. Eco. Prog. Series.*

________, ________, W. Stifel; B.G. Bays; and A. Wollman. 1983. (Abstract) The migratory movement of humpback whales between Hawaii and Alaska. Boston: Fifth Biennial Conference on the Biology of Marine Mammals, Nov. 27–Dec.1.

________, K.J. Krieger, and B.L. Wing. 1985. (Abstract) The energetics of humpback whales, with reference to caloric content and observed densities of prey in Southeastern Alaska. Vancouver, B.C.: Sixth Biennial Conference on the Biology of Marine Mammals, Nov. 22-26.

________, A. Perry, and L.M. Herman. 1985. (Abstract) Reproductive parameters of female humpback whales in the North Pacific. Vancouver, B.C.: Sixth Biennial Conference on the Biology of Marine Mammals, Nov. 22-26.

Barnes, L.G. 1976. Outline of eastern North Pacific fossil cetacean assemblages. *Syst. Zool.* 25: 321-43.

Bauer, G.B., M. Fuller, J.R. Dunn, J. Zolger, and L.M. Herman. 1983. (Abstract) Biomagnetic studies of cetaceans. Boston: Fifth Biennial Conference on the Biology of Marine Mammals, Nov. 27–Dec. 1.

________, L.M. Herman, B.G. Bays, T. Kieckefer, B. Taylor, P. Dawson, M. Veghte, and A. Frankel. 1985. (Abstract) Effects of vessel traffic on the behavior of humpback whales in Hawaii. Vancouver, B.C: Sixth Biennial Conference on the Biology of Marine Mammals, Nov. 22-26.

Beamish, P. 1975. (Abstract) Biology and acoustics of a temporarily entrapped humpback whale. Santa Cruz: Conference on the biology and conservation of marine mammals, Dec. 4-7.

________. 1978. Evidence that a captive humpback whale *(Megaptera novaeangliae)* does not use sonar. *Deep Sea Res.,* 25: 469-472.

Bentley, P.J. 1963. Composition of the urine of the fasting humpback whale *(Megaptera nodosa). Comp. Biochem. Physiol.,* 10: 257-259.

Breathnach, A.S. 1955. The surface features of the brain of the humpback whale *(Megaptera novaeangliae). J. Anat.,* 89: 343-354.

Brown, S.G. 1959. Whale marks recovered in the Antarctic seasons 1955/56, 1958/59, and in South Africa 1958 and 1959. *Norsk Hvalf.Tid.,* 48: 609-616.

Bryant, P., G. Nichols, Jr., T. Boettger, and K. Miller. 1980. Krill availability and distribution of humpback whales in Southeastern Alaska. Boston: Ocean Research and Education Society, expedition #16.

Carlson, C.A., and C.A. Mayo. 1983. (Abstract) Changes in the pigment and scar patterns on the ventral surface of the flukes of humpback whales observed in the waters of Stellwagen Bank, Massachusetts. Boston: Fifth Biennial Conference on the Biology of Marine Mammals, Nov. 27–Dec. 1.

Chabot, Denis. 1985. (Abstract) A quantitative technique to compare and classify humpback whale sounds. Vancouver, B.C: Sixth Biennial Conference on the Biology of Marine Mammals, Nov. 22-26.

Chittleborough, R.G. 1953. Aerial observations on the humpback whale, *Megaptera nodosa* (Bonnaterre), with notes on other species. *Aust. J. Mar. Freshwat. Res.,* 4: 219-229

________. 1955. Puberty, physical maturity, and relative growth of the female humpback whale, *Megaptera nodosa* (Bonnaterre), on the Western Australian Coast. *Aust. J. Mar. Freshwat. Res.,* 6: 315-327.

________. 1957. Breeding cycle of the female humpback whale. *Fish. Newsl.,* 16: 5.

________. 1958. The breeding cycle of the female humpback whale, *Megaptera nodosa* (Bonnaterre). *Aust. J. Mar. Freshwat. Res.,* 9.

________. 1959. Determination of age in the humpback whale *Megaptera nodosa* (Bonnaterre). *Aust. J. Mar. Freshwat. Res.,* 10: 125-143.

________. 1959. Intermingling of two populations of humpback whales. *Norsk Hvalf.Tid.,* 48: 510-514, 517-521.

________. 1965. Dynamics of two populations of the humpback whale, *Megaptera novaeangliae* (Borowski). *Aust. J. Mar. Freshwat. Res.,* 16: 33-128

Chu, Kevin C., and Sharon L. Nieukirk. 1985. (Abstract) Dorsal fin shapes and scars as indicators of sex, age and social status in humpback whales *(Megaptera novaeangliae).* Vancouver, B.C: Sixth Biennial Conference on the Biology of Marine Mammals, Nov. 22-26.

________, C. Mayo, and M. Weinrich. 1985. (Abstract) The effect of whale watching in the southern gulf of Maine on distribution and reproductive rates of humpback whales. Vancouver, B.C: Sixth Biennial Conference on the Biology of Marine Mammals, Nov. 22-26.

Cuccarese, S.V., and D.D. Evans. 1981. The North Pacific humpback whale *(Megaptera novaeangliae):* its status on Alaskan grounds. Report to the Arctic Environmental Information and Data Center, Anchorage, AK.

Darling, J.D. 1978. The winter whales of Hawaii-part one: To Hawaii for the winter. *Waters-J. Van. Aquar.,* 3: 9-18.

Dawbin, W.H., and R.A. Falla. 1957. (Abstract) Changes in parasitic infections during the growth of humpback whales. *Aust. J. Sci.,* 20: 19.

________, and ________. 1959. Evidence on growth-rates obtained from two marked humpback whales. *Nature,* 183: 1749-1750.

________, and ________. 1964. Movements of humpback whales marked in the South West Pacific Ocean 1952 to 1962. *Norsk Hvalf.Tid.,* 53: 68.

Dehalt, Annette C. 1985. (Abstract) An oceanographic interpretation of the humpback whale *(Megaptera novaeangliae)* population decline in Glacier Bay, Southeast Alaska. Vancouver, B.C: Sixth Biennial Conference on the Biology of Marine Mammals, Nov. 22-26.

Dohl, T.P. 1983. (Abstract) Return of the humpback whale *(Megaptera novaeangliae)* to central California. Boston: Fifth Biennial Conference on the Biology of Marine Mammals, Nov. 27–Dec. 1.

Dolphin, W. F. 1985a. (Abstract) Food availability may measurably affect reproductive success in humpback whales. Vancouver, B.C: Sixth Biennial Conference on the Biology of Marine Mammals, Nov. 22-26.

________. 1985b. (Abstract) Sonar and underwater cameras used to examine the foraging of humpback whales. Vancouver, B.C: Sixth Biennial Conference on the Biology of Marine Mammals, Nov. 22-26.

________, and D. McSweeney. 1981. (Abstract) Aspects of the foraging strategies of humpback whales determined by hydroacoustics scans. San Francisco: Fourth Biennial Conference on the Biology of Marine Mammals, Dec. 14–8.

Dudok van Heel, W.H. 1977. Sound and cetacea. *Netherlands Jour. of Sea Res.,* 60: 407-507.

Duffield, D.A.; J. Chamberlain-Lea; W. Gilmartin; I. Kang; and R. Lambertsen. 1985. (Abstract) Chromosomes of the Pacific and Atlantic humpback whale, *(Megaptera novaeangliae).* Vancouver, B.C: Sixth Biennial Conference on the Biology of Marine Mammals, Nov. 22-26.

Earle, S.A. 1979a. (Abstract) Feeding behavior of humpback whales. Abstracts of papers from the proceedings of the 14th Pacific Science Congress, Khabarovsk, USSR, Committee F, Section FIII, 129.

________. 1979b. Humpbacks: The gentle whales. *National Geographic* 155: 2-17.

Edel, R.K., and H.E. Winn. 1978. Observations on underwater locomotion and flipper movement of the humpback whale *Megaptera novaeangliae. Mar. Bio.,* 48: 279-287.

Fanning, J. 1979. (Abstract) The blow of whales—a functional explanation. Seattle: Third Biennial Conference on the Biology of Marine Mammals, Oct. 7-11.

Fleischer, G. 1976. Hearing in extinct cetaceans as determined by cochlear structure. *J. Paleo.,* 50: 133-152.

Forestell, P.H., and L.M. Herman. 1979a. (Abstract) Observations on humpback whale calves *(Megaptera novaeangliae)* in the Hawaiian winter assembly area. *Pacific Sci.,* 33: 120.

________, and ________. 1979b. (Abstract) Behavior of "escorts" accompanying mother-calf pairs of humpback whales. Seattle: Third Biennial Conference of the Biology of Marine Mammals, October 7-11.

________, L.M. Herman, and G.D. Kaufman. 1985. (Abstract) Aerial survey of seasonal trends and population characteristics of humpback whales in the Four-Island region of Hawaii. Vancouver, B.C.: Sixth Biennial Conference on the Biology of Marine Mammals, Nov. 22-26.

________, Maria B. Veghte, and L.M. Herman. 1985. (Abstract) Evidence for visual search by breaching humpbacks. Vancouver, B.C.: Sixth Biennial Conference on the Biology of Marine Mammals, Nov. 22-26.

________, R. Antinoja, and L. Herman. 1977. (Abstract) Organization and behaviors of humpback whales as a function of pod size. San Diego: Proceedings of the Second Biennial Conference on the Biology of Marine Mammals, December 12-15.

Glockner, D.A. 1978. The winter whales of Hawaii - part two: Underwater with mothers and calves. *Waters - J. Van. Aquar.,* 3: 19-25.

________, and S.C. Venus. 1979. (Abstract) Humpback whale *(Megaptera novaeangliae)* cows with calves identified off West Maui, Hawaii, 1977-'78. Seattle: Third Biennial Conference on the Biology of Marine Mammals, Oct.7-11.

Glockner-Ferrari, D.A., and M.J. Ferrari. 1981. (Abstract) Correlation of the sex and behavior of individual humpback whales *Megaptera novaeangliae.* San Francisco: Fourth Biennial Conference on the Biology of Marine Mammals, Dec. 14–8.

________, and ________. 1983. (Abstract) Reproduction, aggression, and sexual activities in the humpback whale. Boston: Fifth Biennial Conference on the Biology of Marine Mammals, Nov. 27–Dec. 1.

________, and ________. 1985. (Abstract) Reproduction, distribution, and conservation of humpback whales in Hawaiian waters, 1975-1985. Vancouver, B.C: Sixth Biennial Conference on the Biology of Marine Mammals, Nov. 22-26.

Hafner, G.W.; C.L. Hamilton; W.W. Steiner; T.J. Thompson; and H.E. Winn. 1979. Signature information in the song of the humpback whale. *J. Acoust. Soc. Am.,* 66: 1-6.

Hain, J.H.W., G.R. Carter, S.D. Kraus, C.A. Mayo, and H.E. Winn. 1980. (Abstract) Feeding behavior of the humpback whale, *Megaptera novaeangliae,* in the continental shelf waters of the Northeastern United States. Boston: Humpback whales of the Western North Atlantic Workshop, November 17-21.

Hall, J.D. 1979. A survey of cetaceans of Prince William Sound and adjacent vicinity -their numbers and seasonal movements. *In:* Environmental assessment of the Alaskan Continental Shelf - final report of principal investigators, Vol. 6. Biological studies. Boulder, CO: Outer Continental Shelf Environmental Assessment Program, Department of Commerce, Department of Interior, p. 631-726.

Hammond, P.S. 1985. (Abstract) North Atlantic humpback whales: Estimating population size from photo-identification data using variations of the Jolly Seber open population model. Vancouver, B.C: Sixth Biennial Conference on the Biology of Marine Mammals, Nov. 22-26.

Hansen, Donald J. 1985. (Abstract) Environmental assessment of the effects of offshore oil development on marine mammals occurring in Alaska marine waters. Vancouver, B.C: Sixth Biennial Conference on the Biology of Marine Mammals, Nov. 22-26.

Herman, Louis M. 1979. Humpback whales in Hawaiian waters: A study in historical ecology. *Pacif. Sci.,* 33: 1-15.

________, and R.C. Antinoja. 1977. Humpback whales in the Hawaiian breeding waters: Population and pod characteristics. *Sc. Rep. Whales Res. Inst.,* 29: 59-85.

________, ________, C.S. Baker, and R.S. Wells. 1979. (Abstract) Temporal and spatial distribution of humpback whales in Hawaii. Seattle: Third Biennial Conference on the Biology of Marine Mammals, October 7-11.

________, C.S. Baker, P.H. Forestell, and R.C. Antinoja. 1980. Right whale *Balaena glacialis* sightings near Hawaii: A clue to the wintering grounds? *Mar. Ecol. Prog. Ser.,* 2: 271-275.

________, and P. Forestell. 1977. (Abstract) The Hawaiian humpback whale: Behaviors. San Diego: Second Conference on the Biology of Marine Mammals, December 12-15.

________, P.H. Forestell, and R.C. Antinoja. 1980. The 1976/77 migration of humpback whales into Hawaiian waters: Composition description. NTIS, PB80-162332.

Herschman, A., (ed.) 1980. Abstracts of papers of the 146th National meeting 308 January 1980 San Francisco, California. Washington, D.C.: American Association for the Advancement of Science, AAAS Publication 80-2.

Hubbs, C.L. 1965. Data on speed and underwater exhalation of a humpback whale accompanying ships. *Hvalrad. Skr.,* 48: 42-44.

Jones, E.C. 1971. A squaloid shark, the probably cause of crater wounds on fishes and cetaceans. *Fish. Bull.,* 69: 791-798.

Jurasz, C.M. and V. Jurasz. 1975. (Abstract) Bubble net feeding of the humpback. Santa Cruz: Conference on the Biology and Conservation of Marine Mammals, December 4-7.

________, and ________. 1977a. (Abstract) Censusing of humpback whales, *Megaptera novaeangliae,* by body characteristics. San Diego: Proceedings of the Second Conference on the Biology of Marine Mammals, December 12-15.

________, and ________. 1977b. (Abstract) Vessel and humpback whale *Megaptera novaeangliae,* interactions. San Diego: Proceedings of the Second Conference on the Biology of Marine Mammals, December 12-15.

________, and ________. 1978. Humpback whales in Southeastern Alaska. *Alaska Geographic,* 5: 116-127.

________, and ________. 1979. Feeding modes of the humpback whale, *Megaptera novaeangliae,* in Southeast Alaska. *Sc. Rep. Whales Res. Inst.,* 31: 67-81.

Katona, S., and S. Kraus. 1979, August. Photographic indentification of individual humpback whales *(Megaptera novaeangliae):* Evaluation and analysis of the technique. NTIS PB-298 740, Report No. MMC-77/17.

Kaufman, Gregory D. 1983. (Abstract) Ecology of humpback whales in American Samoa. Boston: Fifth Biennial Conference on the Biology of Marine Mammals, Nov. 27–Dec. 1.

________, 1985. (Abstract) Photographic fluke and lateral body identification of Australian humpback whales. Vancouver, B.C: Sixth Biennial Conference on the Biology of Marine Mammals, Nov. 22-26.

________, and Peter F. Jenkins. 1985. (Abstract) Comparisons of Australian and Hawaiian humpback whale songs. Vancouver, B.C: Sixth Biennial Conference on the Biology of Marine Mammals, Nov. 22-26.

________, Helen Sneath, and Robert Slade. 1985. (Abstract) Migratory characteristics of East Australian humpback whales. Vancouver, B.C: Sixth Biennial Conference on the Biology of Marine Mammals, Nov. 22-26.

________, and R.K. Wood. 1981. (Abstract) Effect of Boat Traffic, Air Traffic and Military Activity on Hawaiian Humpback Whales. San Francisco: Fourth Biennial Conference on the Biology of Marine Mammals, Dec. 14–8.

________, and ________. 1983. (Abstract) Demographics of Humpback Whales off Southwest Maui, Hawaii. Boston: Fifth Biennial Conference on the Biology of Marine Mammals, Nov. 27–Dec. 1.

________, ________, and P. Forestell. 1983. (Abstract) Induced Changes in Behavior Patterns and Habitat Usage by Humpback Whales off Southwest, Maui, Hawaii. Boston: Fifth Biennial Conference on the Biology of Marine Mammals, Nov. 27–Dec. 1.

Kaza, Stephanie. 1985. (Abstract) Biophylic values of cetaceans. Vancouver, B.C: Sixth Biennial Conference on the Biology of Marine Mammals, Nov. 22-26.

Kellogg, R. 1929. What is known about the migrations of some of the whalebone whales. Annual Reports of the Smithsonian Institution for 1928, pages 467-494.

Kibblewhite, A.C., R.N. Denham; and D.J. Barnes. 1967. Unusual low-frequency signals observed in New Zealand waters. *J. Acoust. Soc. Am.* 41: 644-655.

Krieger, K, and B.L. Wing. 1984. Humpback whale prey studies in Southeast Alaska, summer 1983. Northwest and Alaska Fisheries Center, Auke Bay Laboratory, Auke Bay, AK.

Lawton, W.S. 1979. Progress report on the acoustical and population studies of the humpback whale in southeastern Alaska, 1979. Report to the Northwest and Alaskan Fisheries Center, National Marine Fisheries Service, Seattle, WA.

________, D. Rice, A. Wolman, and H. Winn. 1979. (Abstract) Occurrence of Southeastern Alaskan humpback whales, *Megaptera novaeangliae,* in Mexican coastal waters. Seattle: Third Biennial Conference of the Biology of Marine Mammals, October 7-11.

Lillie, D.G. 1915. Cetacea. British Antarctic Terra Nova Expedition. *Nat. Hist. Rep. on Zoo.,* 1: 85-124.

Mackintosh, N.A. 1942. The southern stocks of whalebone whales. *Discovery Rep.,* 22: 197-300.

Marine Mammal Commission. 1980. Humpback whales in Glacier Bay National Monument, Alaska. NTIS, PB80-141559, Report No. MMC-79/01.

Mate, B.R. 1983. (Abstract) Movements and dive characteristics of a satellite monitored humpback whale. Boston: Fifth Biennial Conference on the Biology of Marine Mammals, Nov. 27–Dec. 1.

Mattila, David K. 1983. (Abstract) Humpback whales off Puerto Rico: population composition and habitat use. Boston: Fifth Biennial Conference on the Biology of Marine Mammals, Nov. 27–Dec. 1.

________, Linda Guinee, and Charles A. Mayo. 1985. (Abstract) Humpback whale songs on Stellwagen Bank, Massachusetts. Vancouver, B.C: Sixth Biennial Conference on the Biology of Marine Mammals, Nov. 22-26.

Matthews, L.H. 1937. The humpback whale, *Megaptera nodosa. Discovery Rep.,* 17: 7-92.

McSweeney, D., W. Dolphin, and R. Payne. 1983. (Abstract) Humpback whale *(Megaptera novaeangliae)* songs recorded on summer feeding grounds. Boston: Fifth Biennial Conference on the Biology of Marine Mammals, Nov. 27–Dec. 1.

Mobley, J.R., and L.M. Herman. 1985. Transience of social affiliations among humpback whales *(Megaptera novaeangliae)* on the Hawaiian wintering grounds. *Can. J. Zool.* 63: 762-772.

________, L.M. Herman, G.D. Kaufman, A. Frankel, and F. Minogue. 1985. (Abstract) Behavioral response of humpback whales to biological and synthetic sound playback in Hawaii. Vancouver, B.C: Sixth Biennial Conference on the Biology of Marine Mammals, Nov. 22-26.

Nemoto, T. 1959. Food of baleen whales with reference to whale movements. *Sci. Rep. Whales Res. Inst.* 4: 149-290

Ogawa, T. 1953. On the presence and disappearance of the hind limb in cetacean embryos. *Sci. Rep. Whales Res. Inst.,* 8: 127-132.

Omura, H. 1953. Biological study on humpback whales in the Antarctic whaling Areas IV and V. *Sci. Rep. Whales Res. Inst.,* 8: 81-102.

Payne, K., and R. Payne. 1985. Large scale changes over 19 years in songs of humpback whales in Bermuda. *Z. Tierpsychol.,* 68: 89-114.

________, P. Tyack, and R. Payne. 1979. (Abstract) Progressive changes in songs of humpback whales. Seattle: Third Biennial Conference on the Biology of Marine Mammals, Oct. 7-11.

Payne, R.S. 1979. Humpbacks: Their mysterious songs. *National Geographic* 155: 18-25.

________. 1979. (Abstract) Humpback whale songs as an indicator of "stocks." Seattle: Third Biennial Conference on the Biology of Marine Mammals, October 7-11.

________, and D. Webb. 1971. Orientation by means of long range acoustic signaling in baleen whales. *An. N. Y. Acad. Sc.,* 188: 110-141.

________, and S. McVay. 1971. Songs of humpback whales. *Science,* 173: 585-597.

Pedersen, T. 1952. A note on humpback oil and on the milk and milk fat from this species *(Megaptera novaeangliae). Norsk Hvalf.Tid.,* 41: 375-378.

Perkins, J.S., and P.C. Beamish. 1979. Net entanglements of baleen whales in the inshore fishery of Newfoundland. *J. Fish. Res. Bd. Can.,* 36: 521-528.

Pierotti, Raymond, Craig A. Swatland, and Paul W. Ewald. 1985. (Abstract) "Brass-knuckles" in the sea: The use of barnacles as weapons. Vancouver, B.C: Sixth Biennial Conference on the Biology of Marine Mammals, Nov. 22-26.

Pike, G.C. 1953. Colour pattern of humpback whales from the coast of British Columbia. *J. Fish. Res. Can.,* 10: 320-325.

Rayner, G.W. 1940. Whale marking. *Discovery Rep.* 19: 245-284.

Rice, D.W. 1977. A list of the marine mammals of the world. NOAA Technical Report. NMFS SSRF-711.

Robins, J.P. 1960. Age studies on the female humpback whale, *Megaptera nodosa* (Bonnaterre), in East Australia waters. *Aust. J. Mar. Freshwat. Res.,* 11: 1-13.

Scammon, C.M. 1869. On the cetaceans of the western coast of North America. *Proc. Natn. Acad. Sci.,* p. 13-69.

Schreiber, O.W. 1952. (Abstract) Some sounds from marine life in the Hawaiian area. *J. Acoust. Soc. Am.,* 24: 116.

Shallenberger, E.W. 1976. Report to Seaflight & Sea Grant on the population and distribution of humpback whales in Hawaii.

________. 1977. Humpback whales in Hawaii - population & distribution. *In:* Oceans '77 conference record, vol. 2, New York: IEEE; Washington, D.C.: MTS.

________. 1977. (Abstract) The effect of human generated activities on the Hawaiian humpback whale. San Diego: Proceedings of the Second Conference on the Biology of Marine Mammals, December 12-15.

________. 1979. Workshop on humpback whales in Hawaii. *Rep. Int. Whal. Com.* 29: 139-140.

Silber, Gregory. 1983. (Abstract) Social phonations and the associated surface behavior of Hawaiian humpback whales *(Megaptera novaeangliae).* Boston: Fifth Biennial Conference on the Biology of Marine Mammals, Nov. 27–Dec. 1.

________. 1985. (Abstract) Non-song sounds and their relationship to surface behavior in the Hawaiian humpback whale *(Megaptera novaeangliae).* Vancouver, B.C: Sixth Biennial Conference on the Biology of Marine Mammals, Nov. 22-26.

________., and D. McSweeney. 1983. (Abstract) A comparison of social phonations of the humpback whale *(Megaptera novaeangliae).* Boston: Fifth Biennial Conference on the Biology of Marine Mammals, Nov. 27–Dec. 1.

Slijper, E.J., W.L. Van Utrecht, and C. Naaktgeboren. 1964. Remarks on the distribution and migration of whales, based on observations from Netherlands ships. *Bijdragen Tot De Dierkunde,* 34: 3-93.

Stump, C.W.; J.P. Robins; and M.L. Garde. 1960. The development of the embryo and membranes of the humpback whale, *Megaptera nodosa* (Bonnaterre). *Aust. J. Mar. Freshwat. Res.,* 2: 365-386.

Symons, H.W., and R.D. Weston. 1957. An underfished humpback population? *Norsk Hvalf.Tid.,* 46: 231-238.

________, and ________. 1958. Studies on the humpback whale *(Megaptera nodosa)* in the Bellingshausen Sea. *Norsk Hvalf.Tid.,* 47: 53-81.

Thompson, P.O.; W.C. Cummings; and S.J. Kennison. 1977. (Abstract) Sound production of humpback whales, *Megaptera novaeangliae,* in Alaskan waters. *J. Acoust. Soc. Am.,* 62:

________, ________, A.J. Perrone, and S.J. Kennison. 1977. (Abstract) Humpback whale sounds in Alaska, Hawaii and Western North Atlantic. San Diego: Proceedings of the Second Conference on the Biology of Marine Mammals, December 12-15.

Thompson, T.J., and H.E. Winn. 1977. (Abstract) Temporal aspects of the humpback whale song. University Park, PA: Animal Behavior Society meeting.

Townsend, C.H. 1935. The distribution of certain whales as shown by logbook records of American whaleships. *Zoologica,* 19: 1-50.

True, F.W. 1904. The whalebone whales of the Western North Atlantic compared with those occurring in European waters with some observations on the species of the North Pacific. *Smithson. Contr. Knowl.,* 33: 1-332.

Tyack, P. 1980. (Abstract) The function of song in humpback whales *Megaptera novaeangliae. In:* Abstracts of papers of the 146th national meeting, 3-8 January 1980, San Francisco, California. A. Herschman (ed.), Washington, D.C.: American Association for the Advancement of Science, AAAS Publication 80-2, p. 41.

________. 1981. Interactions between singing Hawaiian humpback whales and conspecifics nearby. *Behav. Ecol. Sociobiol.,* 8: 105-116.

Walker, Michael M.; Joseph L. Kirschvink; and Andrew E. Dizon. 1985. (Abstract) Associations between cetacean live strandings and geomagnetic field parameters. Vancouver, B.C: Sixth

Biennial Conference on the Biology of Marine Mammals, Nov. 22-26.

Whitehead, H. 1985. Why whales leap. *Scientific American.* March: 84-93.

________. 1985. (Abstract) Spatial organization of the Western North Atlantic humpback whale. Vancouver, B.C: Sixth Biennial Conference on the Biology of Marine Mammals, Nov. 22-26.

Winn, H.E. 1974. (Abstract) Geographic variation and behavior correlates of the humpback whale. Champaign-Urbana, IL: Animal Behavior Society, May 24-27.

________, P. Beamish, and P.J. Perkins. 1979. Sounds of two entrapped humpback whales *(Megaptera novaeangliae)* in Newfoundland. *Mar. Bio.* 55: 151-155.

________, W.L. Bischoff, and A.G. Taruski. 1973. Cytological sexing of cetacea. *Mar. Bio.* 23: 343-346.

________, P.J. Perkins, and T.C. Poulter. 1970. Sounds of the humpback whale. Menlo Park, CA: Proceedings of the 7th Annual Conference on Biological Sonar and Diving Mammals, 7: 39-52.

________, and T.J. Thompson. 1979. (Abstract) Comparison of humpback whale sounds across the northern hemisphere. Seattle: Third Biennial Conference on the Biology of Marine Mammals, Oct. 7-11.

________, ________, W.C. Cummings, J.H. Hain, J. Hudnall, H.E. Hays, and W.W. Steiner. 1981. Song of the humpback whale—population comparisons. *Behav. Ecol. Sociobiol.,* 8: 41-46.

Wing, B.L., and K. Krieger. 1983. Humpback whale prey studies in Southeast Alaska, summer 1982. Northwest and Alaska Fisheries Center, Auke Bay Laboratory, Auke Bay, AK.

Wolman, A.A., and C.M. Jurasz. 1977. Humpback whales Hawaii: Vessel census, 1976. *Mar. Fish. Rev.,* 39: 1-5.

Yablokov, A.V., and G.A. Klevazal. 1969. Whiskers of whales and seals and their distribution, structure, and significance. *Fish. Res. Bd. Can.* Translations Series, No. 1335.

Index

Figures in **bold** type indicate the main references or illustrations for major entries.

ABOUT THE AUTHORS

Gregory D. Kaufman was born in Portland, Oregon, He is president of the Pacific Whale Foundation, a director of the Hawaii Whale-watching Association, and a charter member of the Society for Marine Mammalogy. His doctoral research at the University of Auckland in New Zealand has focused on the population dynamics of humpback whales in the North and South Pacific and analysis of their songs.

Paul H. Forestell is the director of Research and Education for the Pacific Whale Foundation, and received his Ph. D. from the University of Hawaii. He has been a senior research associate at the Kewalo Basin Marine Mammal laboratory, and assistant professor at the University of Hawaii. He has conducted research into learning and memory capabilities of dolphins, and field studies of baleen whales since 1976, and is a charter member of the Society for Marine Mammalogy.

PHOTO CREDITS

Robert Aizuss/Pacific Whale Foundation 44
WWF/Abigail Alling 9
Loraine Belcher/PWF 176(R)
William H. Dawbin 129
Fred Felleman 57(T), 62-63 (T)
Paul Forestell/PWF 89(B)
Lili Hagen/PWF 62(B)
Durant Hembree 17(B)
John Hovancik 82
Gregory D. Kaufman/PWF 17(T) 22, 23, 24, 33, 34, 36, 37, 39, 47, 57(B), 58(T), 60, 63, 66-67, 68(M/B), 69(B), 70, 80, 81, 83(T/M0, 84-88, 89(T), 91-95, 97, 99-101, 104, 107, 109, 111, 113, 122, 123, 124(T), 125, 126, 130-132, 125(R), 152, 153, 156, 158, rear cover
Gregory D. Kaufman/courtesy of the Kewalo Basin Marine Mammal Laboratory 50, 51, 55, 69(T)
The New Zealand Herald 158-159
Flip Nicklin/Nicklin and Associates 16(T/B), 25(B)
Mike Osmond/PWF 25(T), 38, 58(B), 59(T/B), 115-117, 119, 121
Vassili Papastaurou/Galapagos Sperm Whale Project 128
Bill Raney 120(B)
Ed Robinson/PWF 8, 72
Donna Silva 136
Robert W. Slade/PWF front cover, ii, 23(B), 26, 69(M), 83(B), 118, 120(T), 124 (B), 133
Mari Ann Smultea/PWF 62(M), 98
Helen Sneath/PWF 61, 68(T), 96, 112
Helen Sneath/courtesy Kewalo Basin Marine Mammal Laboratory 46
Phillip Stringer/PWF 135(L)
Mason Weinrich/Gloucester Fishermen's Museum Cetacean Research Unit 29, 65
Anne Windsor 15
R. Kevin Wood/PWF 49, 154

ILLUSTRATIONS

Laurence de Betham Anderson 53
Brooks G. Bays Jr. 7, 41, 52, 54, 102-103, 106, 108, 157
Stephen Dawson 10-11, 12, 19, 20-21, 27, 28-29, 30-31, 43, 45, 48, 56, 71, 140-150, 161
Lili Hagen/PWF x, 51, 78, 138
Prints courtesy of Lahaina Printsellers 4, 127

HOW YOU CAN HELP
YOU CAN MAKE A DIFFERENCE!

By supporting the **Pacific Whale Foundation's** vital work to save the whales and their environment.

☐ I WANT TO BECOME A PWF MEMBER!

☐ $15 Senior Citizen/Student
☐ $20 Individual
☐ $25 Family
☐ $30 Foreign
(Outside U.S.A. & Australia)
☐ $50 Institution
☐ $100 Supporting
☐ $250 Contributing
☐ $500 Patron

☐ ENCLOSED IS MY GIFT OF:
☐ $________________
☐ $1000
☐ $50
☐ $500
☐ $100
☐ $25

☐ I WANT TO ADOPT-A-WHALE! Enclosed is my gift of $75 to adopt a
☐ Hawaiian ☐ Australian humpback whale.

Whale's Name ____
An Annual Support Fee of $50 is due after the first year of adoption.

Name(s) ____

Street ____

City ____________________ State ____________ Zip ____________

☐ This adoption or membership is a gift to the following:

Name(s) ____

Street ____

City ____________________ State ____________ Zip ____________

☐ Check enclosed, payable to **Pacific Whale Foundation.**
☐ Charge my VISA ☐ MasterCard

____________________ ________________________________
EXPIRATION DATE SIGNATURE

Your contribution is U.S. tax-deductible.

PLEASE SEND ME INFORMATION ABOUT PWF's:
☐ Research Internship Program
☐ Adopt-A-Whale Program
☐ Marine Expeditions and Events
☐ Gift Catalog

Thank you for your valuable contribution.

Please mail to: **PACIFIC WHALE FOUNDATION**
Kealia Beach Plaza / 101 N. Kihei Road / Kihei, HI, U.S.A. 96753 / 808-879-8811